The Taste of New Wine

Long before *recovery* became a household word, Keith Miller was setting forth a bold message of spiritual renewal through his books and seminars. Now his popular volume *The Taste of New Wine* has been updated for the 1990s.

Keith Miller declares in *The Taste of New Wine*, "God does not want our money, nor does He primarily want our time. ... I believe He wants our permission to come into our lives and show us how to live creatively and freely in loving relationships with Him and people. And if we give Him our permission, He will begin to show us life as we've never seen it before."

This evangelical classic is written in a compelling and honest spirit. Highly readable, practical and motivating, it meets a vital need of all Christians—those new in the faith, those who want to continue to mature and explore spiritual growth, and those who are dissatisfied with their personal relationship with Jesus Christ. And it offers new hope and a sense of freedom and direction for living the Christian life to its fullest.

BY Keith Miller:

A Hunger for Healing: The Twelve Steps as a Classic
    Model for Christian Spiritual Growth
Hope in the Fast Lane: A New Look at Faith in a
    Compulsive World
The Scent of Love
Habitation of Dragons
Please Love Me
The Taste of New Wine

WITH Pia Mellody and Andrea Wells Miller:
Facing Codependence: What It Is, Where It Comes From,
    and How It Sabotages Our Lives

WITH Bruce Larson:
The Edge of Adventure: An Experiment in Faith

KEITH MILLER

THE
TASTE
OF
NEW
WINE

Fleming H. Revell Company
Tarrytown, New York

Library of Congress Cataloging-in-Publication Data

Miller, Keith.
    The taste of new wine / Keith Miller.
        p.   cm.
    Includes bibliographical references.
    ISBN 0-8007-5413-1
    1. Christian life—1980- 2. Miller, Keith.   I. Title.
BV4501.2.M483   1991
248.4—dc20   91-29873
                                                                                CIP

Copyright © 1965, 1991 by Keith Miller
Published by the Fleming H. Revell Company
Tarrytown, New York 10591
Printed in the United States of America

CONTENTS

CONTENTS

PUBLISHER'S FOREWORD

🍇 IN A DAY WHEN SO MUCH WRITING IS about as bland as Velveeta cheese, Keith Miller writes with a convincing vigor and color as he takes us on a spiritual adventure that focuses on the eternal truth of God's love and faithfulness.

In the spirit of another perceptive writer and friend of the author, the late Dr. Paul Tournier of Geneva, Switzerland, Keith Miller offers us "not only his ideas but his person." Indeed, as we read we sense a vibrant truth expressed years ago by Leo Tolstoy, nineteenth-century Russian novelist and social critic; at dinner after some especially productive writing hours, he commented to his family, "Today I left a piece of my life in the inkwell."

Well over 2 million readers have already discovered, since this classic was first published in 1965, that for Keith Miller Christianity is a way of life, not a laundry list of rules and regulations. Nor is it a soothing collection of dogma calculated to provide glib answers to the wrenching questions we all confront in our effort to live productive lives in a complex and modern world.

Rather, *The Taste of New Wine* resonates with a pulsating message of faith that is just as up-to-date and relevant as when these words were first written. Here is a timeless call for spiritual renewal and openness. Here, too, we find helpful and hope-filled guidelines for living in relationship with God and with one another.

We are pleased to publish this updated edition of *The Taste of New Wine*. Indeed, the "wine" is still "new"; its "taste" still carries the promise and challenge of the spiritual resources available to us as we move expectantly through these closing days of the twentieth century and into the opening moments of the twenty-first century.

FOREWORD

In june, 1961, when i went to la-ity Lodge for the initial retreat, I little knew the wealth of human dividends that were in store for me. The finest of these unexpected dividends was the friendship of Keith Miller, whom I then met for the first time. From the beginning it was evident that in this man was the combination of intellectual sharpness and spiritual depth which our time so sorely needs. Subsequent encounters, during the past years, at Earlham College and elsewhere, have verified the original judgment and increased the original hope. And now that the book has been written, I am glad to introduce it to potential readers in this country and abroad.

The book *The Taste of New Wine* is not a book about religion, but rather a work which belongs to the category of witness. Keith Miller does not, primarily, discuss witness; he provides, instead, a firsthand testimony of what has transpired in his own life. The book is an interim report concerning the way in which God has reached him in both pain and joy.

It is an accident that the book makes abundant use of the pronoun "I." There are people who seek, self-consciously, to avoid the employment of this pronoun, but Keith Miller has been wise not to engage in such a futile effort. After all, the most important thing a man has to say is not some speculation about what may be true, but rather a direct and un-self-conscious reporting of what has occurred in firsthand experience. The only testimony which has any value is that which necessitates the first person. It is not possible to find anything more basic than the report of one who says, simply and humbly, "Whereas I was blind, now I see."

There is only one pronoun nobler than "I," and that is "Thou." The author of this book seeks to order his life in direct response to One who is best understood as the Eternal Thou. In short, his religion is centered in prayer and he knows that a man has made a beginning in prayer when, abandoning mere discussion, he sincerely says, "O God, You." When so many are vague on this point, or even impersonal in their emphasis, the words of our author come to us with a refreshing straightforwardness.

Keith Miller's book will, I predict, have a wide and appreciative reading for many reasons, but chiefly because his mood is wholly unapologetic. He takes a stand and he is clear enough to let the reader know what the stand is. There is no person whom I know whose book I should rather recommend than this one.

D. ELTON TRUEBLOOD

PREFACE

It was 1965. FOR THREE YEARS I HAD directed and participated in various conferences at an interdenominational lay center in Southwest Texas called Laity Lodge. I had sensed an exciting new movement of renewal in the lives of Christians all over America; but I had been increasingly concerned about one recurring type of question asked by lay men and women. Most of these people were officers in local Christian congregations; and many had been denominational leaders for years. Yet again and again, when we asked them during a conference to write personal, anonymous questions, they secretly told us that they did not know how to pray, how to witness to other people about Christ without being embarrassed, how to simply communicate with their families, or how to approach their vocational and social lives as committed Christians.

This book was written to these people. It is a distillation of nine years of struggling alone and with small groups to find a way to live and communicate as a layman the amazing power and love inherent in the Christian gospel. There are many ways to discuss the doctrines of Christianity; but when it comes to living the Christian life, I have come to believe that each person has only one story to tell. And recorded here is mine.

Now it is 1991. Through the twenty-six years of happiness and pain since *The Taste of New Wine* was first released, I have realized that what is in this book is true in deeper ways than I could see when I first wrote it. For example, when I said that we Christians are "a dishonest people who often train our children to be dishonest," I didn't realize how much of my own life was hidden from me because of my denial.

God was very gracious to me. The original editions of this book sold an enormous number of copies, and I was asked to speak about faith in Christ and living for Him over several continents and in many countries. I became very busy with my ministry—in fact I worked so compulsively I often couldn't stop. God led me through the pain of realizing that I can't control others, even my family members—and indeed I'm not supposed to. In my frantic working for Jesus I fell into some of the same traps I warned people about in this book, and in 1976 I was divorced.

The reaction of many people in the church to this was to reject me outright. I felt lonely and frightened, like the small child that I am inside, who was always afraid he wasn't good enough. Some Christian men, in a prayer group I attended, held me while I cried and tried to sort out my life. Then I saw a book title that was something like, *The Church Is the Only Army That Shoots Its Wounded.* I said, "Yes!" But in my prayer time God seemed to say to me, "Keith, quit blaming your sin, your bad behavior, and people's rejection of you on the church or anyone else. You face your own issues, and I'll take care of my church."

So I did. I went for treatment and began facing my compulsive and addictive tendencies. I started a new phase in my Christian life, trying to find out how God could best use me now.

God has led me to some new ways to face my own sin and change some of the lifelong patterns I couldn't even see for years. Instead of running from pain and fear, I can often be still and listen, because I now believe that if I will stand in my pain with God and listen to Him and His recovering children, He and they can teach me what I need to learn about God, myself, and loving His people that can give me the serenity to live for Him one day at a time and enjoy the process. I have chronicled some of this pilgrimage in two books: *Hope in the Fast Lane* and *A Hunger for Healing.*

And I have "gone back out" to speak and witness about God's process of recovery for those of us who love Him but have "lost touch" somehow with God and other people—and our own precious inner child.

I am very grateful that Fleming H. Revell is bringing this book out at this time. As I have reread *The Taste of New Wine*, I have found it to be more relevant to me now as I have had a chance to live through more of the pain and joys of trying to be Christ's person in the real world. And now as the Lord and His message have called me out of myself once more to live for Him among His people, I am thrilled to join my friends at Revell in bringing to you *The Taste of New Wine*.

ACKNOWLEDGMENTS

I<small>T IS IMPOSSIBLE TO ACKNOWLEDGE</small> specifically the help of those people whose lives, writings, and counsel over these past years may appear in this book as insights apparently "discovered" by me. I have tried, where practical, to give credit to the original human donor. But I am afraid many of the ideas have been so mingled and integrated that they have become a part of my own spiritual bloodstream. I can only say "thank you" to those of you who may see your influence in print here.

Since I have spoken so often on the same programs with Howard Butt, Jr., and studied with Dr. D. Elton Trueblood, I have probably stolen most freely, though unconsciously, from them. I would never have written this book if it had not been for the encouragement of my teacher and friend, Elton Trueblood, to whom I owe so much—not only for his guidance in my life but for his immediate help and suggestions in reading this manuscript. I would like to thank Mrs. Howard E. Butt, Sr., and Howard and Barbara Dan Butt for encouraging me to do this writing while working as director at Laity Lodge. Also I want to express deep gratitude to Mr. and Mrs. Carl Newton and to Gene Warr who, through their generosity, helped make it possible for me to study at the Earlham School of Religion. Mrs. Bill Lee, who typed the early sketches of this manuscript, gave not only mechanical help but the invaluable support of enthusiasm. I am also indebted to our friend, Gladys Ranger, for her assistance in typing the final copies.

To the editors of the *Review and Expositor* I am grateful for permission to use part of the material appearing here in chapters one and seven which appeared earlier in that journal. Similarly, I want to thank the editors of *Faith at Work* with regard to material found in chapters three and six. Also, grateful acknowledgment is hereby made to the authors and publishers set out in the footnotes and to Mrs. William Temple for permission to quote from the works mentioned in the following pages.

Finally, I owe a deep debt of gratitude to Mary Allen Miller, to whom *The Taste of New Wine* is dedicated.

THE
TASTE
OF
NEW
WINE

CHAPTER ONE

Something is loosed to change the stricken world.
Stephen Vincent Benet

OUT
OF
THE
FERMENT

SEVERAL YEARS AGO I STUMBLED into a new style of life which is flooding into the main stream of the church today. This new life can be seen in the experience and witness of thousands of business and professional men and women and Christian ministers and their families in America today. These people, clergy and laymen, have in many different ways realized some striking facts. For years the New Testament's call for total commitment of the whole person—with his or her vocation, family, and avocations—had been seemingly lost, drowned in the midst of the noises of building a better America, a better world, and ironically a better "church." Thousands of yards of concrete were poured into hundreds of new sanctuaries, parish halls and parking lots. Millions of new people were recruited to membership in church activity. Yet somehow in the process something of the wholeness of Christ slipped through our fingers. An obvious separation was allowed to grow between denominations and an even worse separation between a living faith in any denomination and one's secular vocation. And in some ways most deadly of all was the grayness and lack of freshness in the worship and program of the average church. Where was the enthusiasm of the people if we were really dealing with a God who is alive?

On Main Street the wind of the Spirit grew still, and it is difficult to see where it "listeth" as the concrete of our generation's progress has hardened. In the business and professional worlds' eyes, Christ has been relegated at best to a position of Lord of the specifically "religious" activities. And as an active and dedicated churchman I had seen from the inside that to call the Christ of the New Testament *Lord* of the average congregation's *contemporary activity* in any true sense was preposterous.

Contemporaneously with the recognition of these facts there were indications in dozens of different geographical and ecclesiastical areas of the stirring of a new order of Christians, an order which has transcended denominational and vocational lines and the members of which travel hundreds of thousands of miles a year to encourage each other, to have a living Christian fellowship, and to struggle together with stark and actual problems they face in common.

These men and women are a serious yet amazingly happy band of converted Christian lay people in America. They are alert. Many of them are unusually successful in their secular vocational pursuits. Most are active in their own denomination's witness. Yet there is nothing of the spiritual grayness of the institution about them. They are *alive* in a striking way!

There is no organization; there are no dues, no memberships—in fact there is only one reason they can be called a "band." They have in common only the Lordship of Jesus Christ and a deep conviction that His call is to the *whole person*—vocation and all. When investigated, the only credentials this group can present to their sometimes skeptical denominations are the hundreds of transformed and growing lives in the wake of their witness.[1] They are often disturbing. For these modern disciples are not satisfied with abstract statements of doctrine—however accurate. They feel a strange gap between the church's doctrinal statements and the problems of the marketplace as they *actually are*.

Out of the resulting frustration has come a feeling that the church is too "philosophical" in its orientation and that the philosophic mind easily forgets its base in the actualities

---

[1] "The ultimate verification of our religion consists of the changed lives to which it can point and for which it is responsible." (See D. Elton Trueblood, *Foundations for Reconstruction* [New York: Harper and Brothers, 1961], p. 107.)

of a person's life. It can get lost in abstractions. Søren Kierkegaard said of Hegel that when he asked the philosopher, in effect, for directions to a street address in Copenhagen he was given only a map of Europe.

A map of Europe or any other continent will not do for this pilgrimage. This new order of "live ones" has realized that the universality of Christ's message is only intelligible as it is focused in *specific* lives and *specific* vocational situations which demand specific decisions for or against Christ's will as it can be perceived in the struggles for power, for prestige, and for material goods.

This new fellowship was brought into existence when some deeply concerned lay people found the institutional church defensive concerning the structured programs and in many cases unprepared to face the problems confronting this new body of missionaries—to the specialized vocational life of our generation. Some Baptists, Methodists, Episcopalians, Presbyterians, and Catholics who were trying to commit *their whole* lives to Christ found that they had more in common with each other than with some of the pillars of their own denominations. And the band of disciples includes many people who've found Christ in movements outside the conventional church. Like mushrooms, the Jesus movements, the charismatic groups, the lay witness people, and many others have appeared and become gateways into the larger Body of Christ.

These men and women were not the "Junior-Preachers" of a day gone by. They were not like clerical assistants wanting only more academic knowledge than their fellows about the theology and worship of the church—though they want this too; instead they constitute a new body of disciples concerned about their *love* of God and saying instinctively and from the own experience that "the knowledge of God is very far from the love of Him."[2]

Although many of these business men and women, attorneys, physicians, and politicians are not academically sophisticated in their theological training, they are turning to the Living Christ as their Teacher and to the Bible as a valid revelation of the nature of God and man. Consequently, although they realize the deep need for further knowledge, their lives and their message are close to the heart of the Christian Way as perceived by remarkable Christians of all ages: "The heart of religion is not an opinion about God such as philosophy might reach as a conclusion of its arguments; it is a personal relationship with God."[3] "Faith is not the holding of correct doctrines but a personal fellowship with the Living God. . . . *What is offered to man's apprehension in any specific Revelation is not truth concerning God but the Living God Himself.*"[4]

In their examination of the Scriptures as converted Chris-

---

[2] Blaise Pascal, *Pensées* (E. P. Dutton and Co., Inc., 1958), p. 79.

[3] William Temple, *Nature, Man and God* (London: Macmillan Co. Ltd., 1956), p. 54.

[4] Ibid., p. 322 (Archbishop Temple's italics).

tians, men and women are discovering that institutional churchmanship, as it is commonly known in the United States, simply does not express for them the wholeness of the new life they are experiencing. Christ is tearing out the partitions in people's souls between vocation, church, and home and making a one-room dwelling place for Himself in their whole lives. People are rediscovering that "religion is not a form of experience existing separately from other forms of experience. It is the transfiguration of the whole of experience."[5]

To those of us who are part of this new going forth, there is an excitement akin to that reflected in the Book of Acts. But after the first burst of enthusiasm there have also been questions, serious questions, from church leaders and from those people who are newly involved, both ministers and lay persons, in this evangelical renewal.

What is it about this "new life" which makes its bearers no longer satisfied merely to sit in the pews and on committees or even to stand in pulpits? Why are the old wineskins feeling a disturbing tenseness as the new wine is fermenting? What is this new style of life? What makes the difference?

[5] J. H. Oldham, *Life Is Commitment* (New York: Association Press, 1959), p. 96.

CHAPTER
TWO

❦

The heart is deceitful above all things,
and desperately corrupt;
who can understand it?

Jeremiah 17:9, RSV

A NEW
KIND
OF
HONESTY

DURING MY FIRST FOUR YEARS AS AN active adult churchman I had taught two Sunday school classes, served on numerous committees and on the vestries of two churches. These were fine churches, filled with good, substantial people. But one of the constant sources of frustration was that in Sunday school classes, teachers' meetings, committee meetings, and even vestry meetings in the church there was an amazing lack of basic honesty. It wasn't so much that people lied. We just had an unspoken agreement not to press the truth—when it seemed that the truth might hurt the leaders or someone else's feelings—or really rock the boat. We evidently felt that being honest in such cases would be cruel or tactless. Consequently we lived in a world of subtle duplicity of which we Christians were the contributing cause.

You may say that this does not apply to your church; but I have talked to so many lay people and leaders in the various denominations about this that I am convinced it is almost universally true.

Although I had always tried desperately to be honest and to have integrity, even in the meetings I mentioned, I have only recently realized that *true* honesty has a very deceptive and elusive quality . . . *especially* among those of us who call ourselves Christians. Our tremendous drive for social acceptance and toward conformity in our time is causing us to train our children to be a generation of young liars who do not even realize they are lying. As so many thinking people have pointed out recently, the current and growing moral decay in this country is not so much to be attributed to the underprivileged parent in the slums as to *us*, the middle and upper class American church . . . lay members and ministers.

We train our children to be subtly dishonest almost from the crib. In my mind's eye I can still see a little four- or five-year-old girl sitting in the aisle of a crowded department store several years ago. She was howling with great feeling as her mother was trying to drag her to her feet. She had evidently sat down to play in the dust while her mother was looking at something on the counter. A large man had walked by in the crowded aisle and stepped on the child's hand. Being human, she screamed at the top of her lungs. Everyone looked. What was the mother's reaction? She jerked the little girl up from the floor in embarrassment and said in her ear, "Shh—, don't cry in front of all of these people." I still remember the confused look on the child's face as she stared at her throbbing, swollen hand.

Or, when a little girl is twelve and gets ready to go to a party, what does the mother say? Does she advise her daughter to "Have a good time. Try to look for people who aren't happy and help them to have a nice time too"?

No, she more likely says, "Now listen, honey, if they're not friendly with you, keep smiling. Don't let them know you're unhappy." No, don't let them know that your heart is broken—keep smiling.

So on and on we train our children to *look* happy and successful, to hide their true feelings, their true needs. By the time they are grown, their natural reaction is to put forth immediately the image expected of them in almost any given situation—regardless of how they may honestly feel about that situation.

The result is our churches are filled with people who outwardly look contented and at peace but inwardly are crying out for someone to love them . . . just as they are—confused, frustrated, often frightened, guilty, and often unable to communicate even within their own families. But the *other* people in the church *look* so happy and contented that one seldom has the courage to admit one's own deep needs before such a self-sufficient group as the average church meeting appears to be.

What am I suggesting—that we suddenly drop our masks and reveal ourselves naked to each other and the church with all our secret greed and lust and hate and resentments? No, but I am suggesting that we must realize that our fellowship is incurably crippled until and unless we recognize and face squarely the nature and extent of our deceitfulness with God, with each other, and with ourselves.

I am convinced that although honesty may not be the front doorway to the kingdom of God, it is the *latchstring* to every doorway in His house. And yet, I have found honesty with one's self to be the most elusive state in my own Christian life. Thinking Christians have always been baffled by their own deceitful behavior. In the seventh chapter of Romans, Paul gives us his classic statement of this experience: "I do not understand my own actions. For I do not do what I want, but I do the very thing I hate" (Rom. 7:15, RSV).

The late Archbishop William Temple came very close to the truth, I believe, when he indicated the nature of our deceiving of ourselves. He realized that our *true willing* is what controls our acts. The reason we are disappointed in our actions is because though we consciously wish to be good we really *will* our own self-satisfaction. And until our true willing (which is mostly unconscious) is redirected, we are trapped and don't know why.[1] At this point in his own struggling to try to understand the unreliability of his behavior, Paul cries out, "Wretched man that I am! Who will deliver me from this body of death?" (Rom. 7:24, RSV). Who can let me see who I really am . . . what I in fact really want beneath my valiant words? It seems clear to me now, after years of self-deception as a converted Christian, that the first thing we need to know if we are truly to become new disciples and apostles of our Lord is that through years of habit and reaction to our social milieu we are deeply, though unconsciously, deceptive with ourselves.

To see how this is so, look in any of your areas of temptation (e.g., that one which disturbs you most continually). Of course, if you say you have no temptation, no sin, the New Testament is pretty clear in its witness to the fact that you have already deceived yourself and are void of the truth (1 John 1:8–10). In any case, those of us who have been conscious of temptation, how does it work? What process does one go through in facing an attractive temptation? My own experience has too often been that I say to myself silently, "I don't want to do this thing. I do not want to resent this person, be jealous of that person, or lust for that woman. I do not want to be this kind of a man. I do not want to! Do not want to" . . . and then I succumb and resent them, gossip about them, or lust for them before I

---

[1] William Temple, *op. cit.* See excellent discussion of this point in Lecture IX, "Freedom and Determinism," p. 223 f.

know it. Afterwards I say to God, "I don't know what is the matter with me. I don't *want* to be this way."

But this process and conclusion illustrate the self-deception which tears the rug out from under our relationship with Christ and each other and leaves us disillusioned and bewildered. For I believe the truth of the matter is that at the motivating center of our lives we *really will* to do those things which we do in our weakness. Unconsciously or consciously I deeply want to destroy you with gossip if you have hurt me acutely. I really want to lust for you if you attract me in this way. And *until I see this* I am bewildered by my seeming failure to do what the real me wants to do. I have become convinced that the *real* me is not *failing* but *succeeding* when I succumb to temptation. Because the nature of the real me is to will to gratify my deep egocentric desires.

I (unconsciously) want subtly to control people in a business situation, so I strike back when you threaten to destroy my reputation, my power to control in a committee meeting. If I really wanted only Christ's will (as I claim) then when you remind me in front of a nominating committee that I never get things in on time, I should say, "Thank you for calling this to our attention. I see that it affects the possibilities of my doing as good a job as chairman of this committee as old Joe would. And I think he might do a better job." But this is *not* my reaction. My reaction is one of anger and resentment. I am furious that you have brought to light before this group one of my cardinal weaknesses.

And I submit that we all react this way in certain areas because our real desire is to satisfy our own self-centered needs.

I do not know this because it has been *consciously true.* Because it has not (for the most part). Consciously, as a committed Christian, I have striven to be selfless for Christ. But over these past twenty-two years my day-in, day-out reactions have proved to me time and time again that I actually want my own way more than God's. For example, what else could account for the secret wave of satisfaction I feel when someone who has been opposed to me is discredited or makes a big mistake so that I look better? If I really wanted Christ's will more than my own fulfillment I would be hurt that this child of His was suffering.

Or in my own family, when my wife would put her finger on some uncouth or selfish little habit of mine—if I had really wanted only God's will I would have said, "Thank you, darling, for pointing out this grievous fault in my character; my goal is to eliminate such things." . . . But this was *not* my normal reaction. All of these reactions and many, many more have shown me in living color that my primary and unconscious motivation has been to gratify myself.

But if this is true—that we have really deceived ourselves as committed Christians, why have we done this? And more important—what can we do about it? Indeed, "Who can free us from this body of death?"

The first step for me was to realize starkly and without

excuse that I *have* been dishonest with myself, consciously and unconsciously—and to ask myself why. William Law has said in essence that if a man imputes a selfish motive to his actions every time, he will be correct in an overwhelming number of instances. But why are we so blinded by ourselves? Why can't we just admit that we basically want our own way and that we will go to great lengths to get it? Why do we delude ourselves or pretend that we are such unselfish people?

First, I think we are unreal about ourselves, even as Christians, because we are afraid that if people find out what we are actually like inside, behind the mask, find out that we really don't honestly want to be with them socially as much as we imply, they will not accept us and therefore we won't be able to fulfill our self-centered needs through our associations with them. You think this is too strong an indictment to level at us churchmen? Think it over.

In one's own experience this is very subtle. I believe that many young women join exclusive socio-civic club groups not because of any burning desire to help the helpless, but because (1) it is an honor to be asked. And (2) belonging helps one project an image of benevolence which implies that we are something which we are not—unselfish and deeply concerned about the poor. Of course, there are thousands of exceptions, but the tragedy is that one can even use the term "exception" to describe them.

A more clear-cut example of our dishonesty is our continual tendency to accept social invitations to go places we actually don't want to go to be with people we honestly don't care about being with. When one analyzes *why*, he is drawn to the conclusion that we go for fear we will not be asked back to some more places we do not want to go. And if this rejection took place, we are afraid we might be pushed out of the aura of "their" acceptance which we suspect is the arena of our self-fulfillment.

You may be thinking, "Thank goodness, that is not my problem. I am certainly not dependent on the approval of the crowd for my security." And there have been times when I, too, have reacted against this herd living and become independent. At such times I, too, have said, "Thank God, I'm not in that trap. I don't care what the crowd thinks." But in retrospect I realize that the opinion of those other "independents" to whom I was addressing my remarks meant a great deal to me. I have a friend who is a fine Christian who states publicly that he doesn't care what people think about him; and yet this man cares more than almost anyone I know about what a *select few* people think. He has merely changed the arena and audience on whom he depends for ego-gratification from "the crowd" to a few discerning Christians—but the problem is the same and the unconscious dishonesty with one's self even deeper.

In short, I believe that we deceive ourselves about our selfishness and egocentricity because we are afraid a revelation of our true nature would alienate us from our chosen associates. Further, we cannot face the Bible's implication that the true nature of man is such that each of us is really engaged (however unconsciously) in the building of the kingdom of Keith or Joe (or whatever *your* name is). We must find an appropriate audience because a kingdom with no subjects to respect the king is untenable. (And this is true whether one is a man or woman or whether one's audience is a national one or only a single husband, wife or child.) To build up our images, and our kingdoms, we are subtly dishonest about any thoughts or desires or habits we have which do not fit our projected image for fear our subjects will discover our secret: that inside, behind the façade, we are not really kingly or queenly at all; but instead, in our intimate actions we are the servants, the slaves, of our resentments, our jealousies, our lusts, and our anxieties and insecurities. The more kingly, the more self-sufficient an image we try to project, the more we must dishonestly deny in a hundred ways that we are self-centered little children at heart bent on our own self-gratification.

Although Paul and the other New Testament writers had not heard of Freud's discovery of the unconscious and were therefore not looking for symptoms of its activity among Christians, the very presence and content of the Epistles show clearly that these writers were well aware that the secret self-centeredness of a person does not automatically end when he or she consciously becomes a member of the church. We in the modern Protestant world have somehow intimated that because Christ has overcome our basic sinful condition, our basic separation, an intelligent intellectual assent by us to that proposition in joining the church is supposed to make us automatically God-centered and not self-centered people.

Consequently our modern church is filled with many people who look pure, sound pure, and are inwardly sick of themselves, their weaknesses, their frustration, and the lack of reality around them in the church. Our non-Christian friends feel either "that bunch of nice untroubled people would never understand my problems"; or the more perceptive pagans who know us socially or professionally feel that we Christians are either grossly protected and ignorant about the human situation or are out-and-out hypocrites who will not confess the sins and weakness our pagan friends know intuitively to be universal.

So the new style of life being experienced in the church today begins, I believe, with a new kind of honesty—an honesty which really *believes* that *all* of us have sinned and fallen short of the glory of God. We believe that our nature is to be so centered in ourselves that even as committed Christians "we deceive ourselves and the truth is not in us." And by recognizing that all our efforts and enterprises both in and out of the church are tainted to the core with self-centered desires for recognition, power, or social acceptance, we can come to God anew as helpless little children. In honest confession and acceptance of His perception and power we can begin *now* to live together the abundant life of freedom and openness Christ came to bring all who would come to Him in this way.

And we can begin to live this life not in some far-off time or condition but in the present moment . . . in the *now*. But we must make a new beginning.

CHAPTER THREE

. . . if any one is in Christ, he is a new creation; the old has passed away, behold, the new has come.

2 Corinthians 5:17, RSV

A NEW
KIND
OF
BEGINNING

How does one describe a new beginning with God as the motivating center of his life without basing his description on some vague mystical feeling? How does an individual who wants to have intellectual integrity describe the experience of encountering God as the personal, the immediate and limitless *Thou* in life? The attempt to explain this unfolding in a person's experience is complicated by the fact that Christ did not leave a reasoned theological explanation. All He seems to have pointed to and promised His followers was a *"way"*—a way across the chasm between God and man, between persons . . . and between a person and his real nature.

The gospel of Jesus Christ calls for a different understanding of the nature of truth than most of us have been educated to have. Where the scientific method has been dominant in a Christian lay person's education, he sometimes thinks of God as a Master Thinker, or Philosophical Theologian. In a real sense I believe God is presented in the Christian revelation as more of a living and creative artist than a philosopher or theologian. A philosopher in order to be universal presents an argument or dialogue covering every possible contingency; but an artist in attempting to be universal is terribly specific. For example, to describe the universal experience of frustration, or of questioning about life, a poet gives us a picture of one specific mouse in a field, one Grecian urn, one country churchyard . . . and in these specific scenes or experiences all men can see frustration, and the basic mystery of their own lives.

Christianity says that when God wanted to convey the truth about His infinite love for all people He made that love incarnate in a *single* life . . . and in the action of that life all kinds of people have been able to perceive His love's universal extent through the enlightening work of God's Spirit.[1] History has shown again and again that in trying to

---

[1] I'm aware of the controversy in the church regarding the gender of God, but though I believe strongly that the feminine, intuitive, and creative aspects of God's nature have been grossly neglected, I have chosen here to follow the biblical use of the pronouns.

transmit the essence of the *Life* Christ demonstrated and continues to offer each of us, we cannot speak adequately in propositional terms. We are forced to turn to the language of living experience. In the last analysis we are all reduced to the witness of "that which we have seen and heard" in our own lives.

I do not know any "general rules" for living life as a business man, father, and husband consciously committed to the Living Christ. I know of no scholars in this field. All I can do is to witness to insights received on one adventure of faith which continues to change my own life and that of my family. The fact that these insights have been verified in the Scriptures, in the lives of Christians in the church's history, and in the experience of dozens of contemporary men and women who have come to Laity Lodge has made me believe that they represent more than a subjective pilgrimage. This is the way it began:

By the time I was eighteen years old I was a great success. (At least at the time it seemed that I was.) In a large high school I had won honors in basketball, dramatic reading, and class plays. I had been elected president of the senior class, and finally king of the school. Life's opportunities appeared to be limitless, in spite of the fact that it was 1945 and we were in the midst of the Second World War.

Three months after graduation, I saw the Western world sitting on the brink of an explosion of joy and relief, anticipating momentarily the official word that the war was over.

But fifteen days before the war ended we received word that my only brother, whom I idolized, had been killed in a plane crash while serving in the Air Force. That night I remember sitting alone on the back steps in tears.

We had always been a close family, and my mother's reaction was one of deep grief, as was my father's. As I sat there terribly alone, I felt that someday I had to find the meaning of life. I felt that I had to pour myself into it twice as much, since Earle would not get a chance to live it at all. During those next few months my mother got continually worse, and finally had a nervous breakdown a little over a year later. The strain on my father had been too much also, and at about the same time he had a heart attack. I had left for the Navy two weeks after my brother's death; and after eleven months in the Navy, I had been released to go to college. My parents were sick; and as I began to get to know them as one adult knows others, they poured out their souls separately before me. I realized that although I had been living with them nineteen years, I did not really know these people—nor did they know each other. They did not realize the anguish caused by the little things in their lives which hurt and frustrated each other; and I felt that neither actually understood about the hopes and dreams in the other's soul . . . and yet we had been a close family and had known much love and happiness. I began to realize that there was a great deal of life which I had not counted on.

I went to college on a basketball scholarship and the G.I. bill. During the Christmas vacation of my sophomore year

I was traveling across the state to a fraternity party. We were driving very fast when the right front wheel slipped off onto the highway shoulder which had been washed away. The driver tried to turn the car suddenly back onto the highway, and it went completely out of control. There was a long screech, and I closed my eyes.

Suddenly, I felt like a rock in a tin can as we bounced and rolled 270 yards down a long hillside, over and over, five and a half times. When the car stopped, it was on its side and I was on my face against the groundward side. There was dust everywhere. I lay still for a moment and then opened my eyes. There, beside me was a pair of legs, and I thought my friend who had been riding with me in the back seat had been cut in two. But then the legs began to move and I realized he had been thrown face first out of the rear view window and was struggling to pull his legs free.

When he got out and turned around, he smiled. His face seemed to sort of fall apart from the impact. Blood was covering his face and neck.

I tried to get up on my hands and knees but my head fell, and I realized that I had broken my neck. I kept trying to think, "What happens to you when you break your neck?" All I could remember was that you died. Somehow I wanted to get out of that car to die.

It was just about sunset, and the cold grayness of December was closing in around us. I told my friend what had happened, and then asked him if he could help me get out. He was unhurt except for facial cuts. So I held my head with both hands, realizing that I had to keep my spine straight, and he dragged me out of the car. I remember as he was trying to help me, looking around and seeing spectators standing around the car watching, afraid to help for fear of becoming involved. One man was even taking a photograph, and I thought to myself, "What a cold bunch of —— these are!"

My friend, Bob, put his overcoat on the ground and helped me lie down beside the road, then covered me with my own. I lay there an hour and a half waiting for the ambulance. I remember lying beside the highway and praying simply. I was very much awake. As I prayed I had a strange feeling of peace that permeated my consciousness. I thought to myself, "What a shame to find out so late in my life that this kind of peace is a reality." For the first time I was not afraid to die. I realized at that moment that even in this tragedy which might be the end of life for me there was Something very personal, very real, which was more important than anything else I had ever known.

But I got over the broken neck . . . and the feeling of peace.

The next couple of years were filled with turmoil inside, and yet a turmoil mingled with a great deal of joy. For although I was bearing the burdens of the family in trying to keep my parents afloat emotionally and spiritually as their lives were drawing to an end, I also found and fell in love with a girl at school. Her love changed my life. Although I had recovered from the broken neck I had also pushed God back into the corner of my life as I re-entered the stream of competition for grades and attention. Except that by now a lot of that frantic life had lost its savor. Some of the fresh naivete had been replaced by methodical knowledge of how to get things done in the world of people. In my sophomore year I was elected president of my fraternity, and the same month found out that I was on the verge of having ulcers.

Not many months later I remember sitting in a hospital room, beside the bed of my father, who was dying. I was praying again and wringing my hands in helpless frustration. His stomach ulcers had perforated, and because of his heart condition they could not operate. I was sitting beside his bed watching him bleed to death internally. I loved him very much. As I sat there helplessly shaking my head, a small Roman Catholic nun, one of the Sisters at the hospital, came into the room. She walked over to the other side of my father's bed, picked up his hand and patted it. She said to him gently, "Can you hear me?"

He said, "Yes," very weakly.

She said to him. "Have you ever accepted Jesus Christ as your Lord and Savior?"

He shook his head, "No."

Then she asked him quietly and matter of factly. "Would you like to do this?"

There was a pause, and then he said, "Oh *yes*."

She said to him. "Then repeat after me: I accept you, Jesus Christ, as my Lord and Savior."

He did, and then he twisted in the bed and died.

*　　*　　*

After my father's death I graduated from college and went to work for a major oil company. I had married Mary Allen in my senior year. We were sent to that company's exploration office in Southwest Texas, near the Rio Grande valley, In those next months as I drove through that vast desert land near the Mexican border, I came to love the silence, the stillness, and the vastness very much. I became fascinated by the changes in the desert. The white, hot noonday blast with the heat waves rising continually and visibly off the highway ahead and off the desert to the side would change into an amazing coolness. The magnificent sunsets hinted at something wonderful and very real beyond the horizon. Then suddenly the total blackness of night and coldness would envelop it all. As I drove through that vast desert country alone, day after day, I began to sense something of the majesty and the silent power of God in the world. There awoke in me a realization that I must somehow learn more about God and find out about Jesus Christ—who was supposed to *be* God.

This restlessness grew until one night at home in the middle of the night I woke my wife and said, "Honey, I've got to go back to school to find out about God."

She was sleepy and surprised, but after a moment said, "I'll go with you, but how will we do it?"

We had a new baby and some debts to pay. I said I didn't know but thought maybe we ought to pray about it and we did. I did not have any desire to become an ordained minister but that seemed to be what the kind of interest I had pointed to. This seemingly was what one did when his commitment and interest reached a certain point.

I enrolled in a graduate theological school, realizing that God, that Reality, must lie in this direction. The church said that it did and the world thought that it might.

When the men at the oil company office found out that I was going to study theology many of them did not know quite how to react. I was the first person from that particular office to go to divinity school. They didn't know how to send me off. They had a way which was standard for sending people off to other offices. They didn't know if this would be appropriate. But since there was no precedent for a change, the final social functions engineered by our friends were empowered by the usual spirits, and some of our friends really "tied one on."

I remember one of my closest friends at the office putting his arm around my neck and leaning rather heavily on me about two o'clock one morning and saying to me through deeply sincere and slightly watery eyes, "Buddy, you'll never make it!" And with this send-off we went to live in the East.

But regardless of any preparation we had had, when we got to the school I soon sensed that for me there was something terribly wrong at divinity school. Some of these young men seemed more full of themselves than had the men at the fraternity to which I belonged. There seemed to be an intellectual competitiveness that was very keen, and somehow unloving. But this I understood, and began to try to compete with the best of them. As the weeks rolled by I felt in my soul that this couldn't be the answer to life, since it was only a religious version of the same kind of competitiveness which I already *knew* did not end in Reality. Some of the boys began to talk about being ordained, and their interests were in some cases focused on things I considered to be quite trivial . . . how long must one's surplice be . . . whose wife could make the most beautiful stoles for the various seasons of the year—none of which I could care less about!

When I had arrived at school I didn't know the *answers* to the theological questions we were trying to discuss, but I did know the *questions* people ask when they're dying and when they are afraid. And if God through the church didn't have the answers to these questions, then how could He be God? I wanted to know how people could get to *know* God *personally* in such a way that they could have something of the Holy Spirit in their lives.

I felt that ministers should know God so well that when they came into someone's living room they could almost sit down quietly and open their souls in such a way that God's love in the minister's life would create a real hunger for Reality in the souls of the other people there and lead them to God too. I sensed intuitively that there must be a way to introduce God into other people's lives . . . that this must somehow be what it's all about. But everywhere I found that people wanted to intellectualize the Good News, wanted to make it conceptual or make it propositional and in any case to stay away from personal confrontation. And somehow in those intellectualized arguments, the aliveness of God would evaporate, only to come back into my soul when I was alone in prayer.

I studied hard and was as interested as any other student in the academic work; but I was repelled by the lack of gut-level engagement with the problems of the rawness of living out one's days and nights as a business man, husband and citizen. I felt we were dealing with the awesome God of Moses and the Intellectual Power of the Greeks; but nowhere did I see the personal redeeming God of Jesus Christ.

After four terms of this I realized that whatever was the matter (I did not know), I could not in good conscience be ordained. Our second child was born that fall after my third term. Mary Allen almost died following the birth of this baby. She was desperate and lonely, 1300 miles from home; and I was very little help. I was in a state of turmoil inside that no one knew about, and I began to fear for my sanity. I was trying to take care of our two babies and go to classes. Mary Allen was in the hospital, very sick and frightened. Inside, my soul was like a tableau of warriors by Michelangelo, the figures twisting and turning for release. Finally I realized I had to get out of there. I completed the term, and we left.

The oil company had said we could come back if I ever wanted to work for them again, and I called. They were very kind, but suddenly I realized something for the first time: when a young man in our generation goes off to the ministry, although most of his contemporaries don't really understand, they think it's fine for him. But when he comes back, having left the seminary, they don't understand.

Because of my tremendous self-centeredness and pride, I have always tried desperately to be understood. The oil company took me back and sent us to an office we had been in before. I would rather have gone to almost any other place, because this "going back" represented my first great human failure. There was no way I could explain to the people around me what had gone on and was going on inside my soul, behind the confident mask I showed to the world. I began to work, because I had a wife whom I loved very much and two babies I loved deeply. But there seemed to be no hope, no ultimate purpose any more. If there was a God, the people at the seminary had subtly hinted that I must have turned away from Him (or perhaps this was my imagination). At any rate I felt things closing in on me in the inner chamber of my life.

I used to walk down the streets, I remember, and suddenly would break out in a cold sweat. I thought I might be losing my mind. One day it was so bad that I got in my company car and took off on a field trip alone. As I was driving through the tall pine woods country of East Texas I suddenly pulled off beside the road and stopped. I remember sitting there in complete despair. I had always been an optimistic person, and had always had the feeling that there was "one more bounce in the ball." After a good night's sleep, or perhaps a couple of martinis and a good night's sleep, one could always start again tomorrow. But now there was no tomorrow in my situation. I was like a man on a great gray treadmill going no place, in a world that was made up of black, black clouds all around me.

As I sat there I began to weep like a little boy, which I suddenly realized I was inside. I looked up toward the sky. There was nothing I wanted to do with my life. And I said, "God, if there's anything you want in this stinking soul, take it."

That was years ago. But something came into my life that day which has never left. There wasn't any ringing of bells or flashing of lights or vision; but it was a deep intuitive realization of what it was God wanted from me, which I had never known before. And the peace which came with that understanding was not an experience in itself, but was rather a cessation of conflict. I realized then that God does not want our money, nor does He primarily want our time, even the whole lifetime a young seminarian is ready to give Him. I believe He wants our permission to come into our lives and show us how to live creatively and freely in loving relationships with Him and people. And if we give Him our permission, He will begin to show us life as we've never seen it before.

It *is* like being born again. I saw that I had not seen Christ at seminary because I had never known God personally.

As I sat there I continued to cry, only now the tears were a release from a lifetime of being bound by myself, by the terrific drive to prove that I was something—*what* I had never quite understood. Although I could not understand nor articulate for many months what had happened to me, I knew to the core of my soul that I had somehow made personal contact with the very Meaning of Life.

I started the car and turned toward home.

CHAPTER
FOUR

. . . and the two shall become one. This is a great mystery. . . .

See Ephesians 5:31–32

MARRIAGE . . . CHRISTIAN MARRIAGE

TO SAY THAT LIFE SUDDENLY BE-
came a joyous religious dream might make a better story,
but life did not. As a matter of fact, my first act after driving
home from this commitment encounter was to pour myself
a tall Scotch and water and think it over. Something had
happened to me inside which both frightened and excited
me. It was as if my swollen soul had been lanced and the
poison drawn out; and I was clean. I had a new chance at
life in a way I did not understand but felt deeply to be true.
I didn't dare tell my wife for fear she would think I had
snapped mentally. When this thought occurred to me I
burned my journal describing the hell of the previous

months, because I was afraid I *might* be mentally in trouble and this information might be used to have me committed someday. For the first time since I was a child I had a perspective of hope and challenge and completeness . . . a sense of direction.

At that time I remembered when I was a small boy waking up early on spring mornings and smelling the freshness of the earth and dreaming about those things life might have in store . . . even that day. Then, as I had grown up, I had "put away childish things" and had learned that life was hard and one did not live in continual expectancy. But now, as a grown man with a family, I began waking up and smelling the earth again. Life became animated and real . . . although it began to happen in a way I would never have expected—given my religious preconceptions of what an honestly committed Christian life might be like.

The first inner change I can remember in those beginning months was that I started perceiving things I had never seen before in my own life and in the lives of everyone around me. It was almost as if God had issued me a new set of spiritual eyes. I was both horrified and fascinated at what I saw. For instance, from the time I can remember I had always been trained to be a humble, thoughtful, but hard-driving person. I had been kind to people and consciously felt very unworthy of all the little honors and attentions I had received along the way. But later, when I had been married a few months, I noticed that my wife did not see me as the unselfish person other people had intimated I was. In fact she seemed to sense a great deal of *raw selfishness* in my makeup. I was, of course, keenly disappointed—because it was rather obvious to me that she (though sweet and loving) was a spoiled and self-centered little girl!

But now suddenly as I looked at my life from this new perspective I saw that all of my goodness and thoughtfulness to people—though consciously sincere for the most part— was a part of my overall life's mission . . . to build an unequaled reputation as a fine successful Christian-type man. Unconsciously I had needed to be right so much that I had paid an amazing price in terms of personal time spent being thoughtful to people. What I now saw which horrified me was that the only thing wrong with my life's plan was that (contrary to all my conscious beliefs) it was *totally self-centered*. It was totally calculated to bring honor to myself . . . though directed toward helping others. I realized with amazement that I am almost a complete egoist.

The next startling discovery I made was that I was basically a coward. This was a real blow; and my mind quickly marshaled dozens of acts and situations which belied this terrible revelation. But I knew it was true, though I had not consciously known before.

With these newly seen facts about myself came the realization that this combination (egoism and cowardice) is not only not uncommon even among Christians, but is in fact almost a formula for "success" in this country. From the time I was a small boy playing football I can remember tackling boys much larger than myself with great viciousness. My ego was so great that the opinion of the men and boys watching actually meant more to me than my physical well-being. I hit hard, not because I was tough—but in order to make sure no one would ever know that down inside I might not want to hit them at all.

In college I didn't stay up all night studying for final examinations because I had an insatiable hunger for a knowledge of economics. I stayed up all night to make sure that I *did not fail.* This combination forces a person to pay the price, whatever it is, for outward success and acclaim . . . but it doesn't make for much of a life inside, behind the mask where we really live. One finds he is always "putting out fires" which might shed light on his true insecurity. But these basic faults in my makeup, even though I had not consciously faced them before, had actually worked to my apparent benefit all my life . . . that is, until I got married.

As I have stated, my young wife spotted at least my egoism right away. (It is not difficult to realize whether one's mate's attention is really focused on his or your interests.) I had hidden this self-centeredness so carefully from myself that I would fly into a frustrated and righteous rage when she would come close to revealing it to me. But after five years of marriage God was letting me see my own life and our marriage in a totally new light. I began to realize that I had never truly known what Christian marriage is. Oh, I could have said some doctrinally correct things about Christian marriage . . . a good many. But I couldn't seem to live them out at our address on a day-in-day-out basis. Now I began to discover existentially some strange things about marriage.

To begin with I saw that in marriage there is shared by the partners something analogous to that inmost secret consciousness in one's own deeply personal experience (which I have called the soul). There is an inner life in a marriage—a life which is lived out when two marriage partners are together with no one else present. This private relationship I shall call the soul of a marriage. And this intimate arena can be more carefully recognized than you might think. There is a specific tone of voice people use. Sometimes a huge booming, business tycoon's voice may take on a whining nasal quality in the intimate encounter with his wife in the soul of their marriage. The pillar of the "woman of the church" who is all sweetness and light to the outer world, may turn into a hissing caustic hussy in the private arena of her marriage. There is a definite and highly communicative language marriage partners share at this level in their relationship—much of it unspoken. Each partner has a whole repertoire of "glances." A woman has her "angry" look; a man has his "I hate your guts" look. Or there is the "you're drinking too much, George" look. I have seen a woman nail her husband with a silent glance thirty feet across a crowded cocktail party . . . and watched him wilt as they shared the message intimately in the soul of their marriage . . . surrounded by a hundred oblivious people. The soul of a marriage can be a trysting place where two people can come together quietly from the struggles of the world and feel safe, accepted, and loved . . . or it can be a battleground where two egos are locked in a lifelong struggle for supremacy, a battle which is for the most part invisible to the rest of the world.

Another thing about this area of married life is that we soon place some articles of "furniture" in the soul of a marriage: some resentments, some jealousy, some situations which can be counted on unfailingly to bring anguish. These things begin to clutter up the soul of a marriage almost from the first night.

With this picture of the inner married life in mind, the basic practical problem of a marriage now seems to me to be this: two fine healthy young people wake up one morning and find themselves alone together in the soul of their marriage . . . . realizing that they really don't know each other at all. What has happened is that each partner has come into the marriage with his own vision of what a marriage ought to be.

A girl's vision of a husband depends on many things—what her father was like (and whether she idolized him or despised him), what novels she has read, what movies she has seen, or what TV heroes she's drooled over. All of her impressions of the ideal man for her, unconsciously for the most part, go into a composite image which she dreams her marriage partner will fulfill. A man's vision of a wife evolves in a similar fashion. In retrospect I think Mary Allen's vision of a husband was a perfectly balanced blend of Kevin Costner, Woody Allen, and St. Augustine.

But in all honesty I think my premarital vision of an ideal wife was probably a combination of Mother Teresa, Julia Roberts, and . . . Julia Child. But, of course, a wife not only has a vision of what a husband should be like, she also has a vision of what a *wife* should be. Any similarity between the husband's vision of an ideal wife and the wife's vision of an ideal wife is a rare and beautiful coincidence.

These different visions of the roles of each partner in a marriage constitute a good bit of the material for the frustrating struggles in the soul of the marriage. Many times the wife-to-be may have seen some basic difference in her vision of a husband and the actual man she is about to marry. But the aura of romance (or the confidence of many American women) makes her feel that she can change the actual man to fit the mental image, thus making her total acceptance of him *conditional* . . . a fact which though unconscious to her becomes apparent to the husband quickly in a marriage's soul. Besides this, the young man may have been counting on the wife's changing to his vision. So what do we have?—*two* creators, *two* gods, in the soul of one marriage . . . each vying, each insisting on the validity of his own created image of what a husband and wife, what a marriage ought to be.

So the invisible battle lines are drawn across the soul of a marriage and the siege begins. This is not to say that there is not a great deal of happiness (physical and otherwise) in such a marriage. But in its soul there is at best a peaceful coexistence between two wills, a sort of stalemate with little pockets of resentment and hurt.

This is, I am convinced, an X-ray picture of many marriages within the leadership groups of Protestant churches in every city. And although the first five years of our marriage were, I had thought, the happiest of any couple I knew, the above description in many respects was a picture of our marriage from my perspective. For five years our relationship had been a good one with a lot of happiness and love and with a reasonably workable truce in its soul with regard to the battle of the wills. But our visions of marriage differed in several important respects.

For one thing, my wife had been raised in a family with five daughters and no sons. Her father was of the old Southern school and didn't believe in men helping around the house with dishes, etc. But he made one concession in that he would take the trash basket in the kitchen out and empty it each evening for Mary Allen's mother. I had been raised with only one brother. My father was also of the old Southern background and he did not believe in helping with little household chores either . . . *especially* things like emptying the *trash basket*. And so when we got married and came home from our honeymoon, my bride announced happily, "Honey, unlike some of my friends, I don't want you to dry the dishes and mop the floors or make beds. These things are woman's work." I was about to pop with pride and thanksgiving, when she continued, "But I would appreciate it if you would take the trash basket in the kitchen out and empty it in the evenings."

I was stunned. I realized this was a very crucial point affecting my vision of a man and a husband. This was long before the major accomplishments toward the awareness of sexual equality.

"Honey, I'm sorry," I said slowly, "but I'm *not* taking out that wastebasket. That's woman's work."

Now *she* was stunned . . . and a little angry.

"That's *all* I'm asking you to do!" she said in amazement.

"Honey, I'll work at night and *hire* someone to help you," I said determinedly, "but I'm not taking out that wastebasket." So the wastebasket in the kitchen became the first article of furniture in the soul of our marriage, which had to be stepped around almost daily in our relationship. (Don't laugh; we were in another world in 1949, and your marriage must have something like this. Maybe it's the toothpaste tube—you may be a "roller" and she a "squeezer.")

Another thing that characterized our marriage relationship was that I was almost always convinced that I was right, when we had arguments. I always had a justification for everything I did. Oh, I had given in all right—for strategic reasons—but I had felt very big about doing so.

With all of these little things, however, we had a fine marriage. I suppose (in retrospect) we were just trying to take the rough edges off of each other in the soul of our marriage . . . with sandpaper. But then, five years later, I had gotten to the end of my mental rope that day beside the road in East Texas.

As I began to see the enormity of my ego and the subtlety of my selfishness, I soon had to bring this new perspective and knowledge into the soul of our marriage.

It happened like this: We were arguing about something (not long after I had tried to offer my life to God) and at the height of the disagreeing Mary Allen shook her head and said (as she had a thousand times) in that discouraged tone I knew so well, "Honey, you are *wrong!*"

Ordinarily this would only have spurred me on to further justification of my point. But this time I stopped and thought about what she was trying to tell me. After a few seconds I said slowly, "Honey, I believe you are right. I think I *am* wrong."

Amazed, she looked at me cautiously to see if something sarcastic was coming; and when it didn't, she said, a little confused, "Wait a minute; maybe *I'm* wrong."

This may not sound like much to you. But it was the beginning of a whole new kind of life in the intimate soul of our marriage. For the first time I didn't need so desperately to be right . . . to be the victorious hero in all the encounters in our relationship. I could relax more often and begin to be myself. I suppose this new commitment I was trying to live would have been all right with my wife (she certainly liked the changes in me) . . . except for one horrible mistake I made: I tried to convince her that *she* should do the same thing. On the surface it sounds perfectly logical that a husband who had been deeply converted to a Living Christ should go about trying to get his wife equally converted. I am convinced that this is not only wrong, but that it is one of the unnecessary sources of deepest anguish in marriages in which only one partner is really trying to commit his or her life to Christ.

From *my* perspective I was trying to tell my wife that I had found something wonderful—a freedom and sense of reality I'd never known was possible for people like us. But strangely, my most enthusiastic witnessing made her very cool and upset. I couldn't understand it. Later she told me that from *her* perspective all she could hear me saying those days beneath my words was that we had been happily married for five years and now suddenly I didn't like her as she was. I was not going to accept her fully any more unless she *changed* into some kind of religious fanatic (or changed somehow in a way she didn't know how to change). I was threatening her very life and our life together . . . and of course I didn't even realize it, since I was saying such "good, true things." So, in her rebellion, she had begun subtly to point to areas in my life wherein if I were such a committed Christian, why was it that I "still reacted in the same old way"?

In my frustration I began to try to convince her that God had really changed me. In looking around for something to do to prove that I had changed, I did as many well-meaning Christians do when they are trying to convince someone close to them that they are different; I fastened onto something I liked to do, I decided to be more loving physically.

There is nothing wrong with being more loving . . . except that at that time it made me happier instead of her. A dear friend of ours in New York finally brought home the stark fallacy of my secret campaign by telling me what his wife used to do when she wanted to convince him that she was a good Christian wife or that she was sorry for some selfish behavior. She would bake him a pie. She loved to bake and was a terrific cook. The only trouble was that my friend didn't like pies; he wanted her to make love to him.

While I was looking around for some other way to convince my wife that I had really changed, my glance fell on the wastebasket standing full by the back door. "No, Lord," I groaned quietly to myself, "not the wastebasket! Take my income, anything." But I suddenly knew that for me it had to be the wastebasket. Without saying a word I took it out, and didn't even mention it to her. (I had emptied it before in order to manipulate her into doing something I wanted to do. But not this time.) I began to really make an effort to take the trash out every day because I realized *that this was where my pride was fastened.* And I think this was when Mary Allen knew that something had really happened in my soul. I learned through this experience to look at the grubby little resentments and in areas where I am deeply defending my position to find really convincing ways to express the selfless love of Christ in my intimate human relationships with those people who truly know me.

Finally I realized the un-Christian pressure my trying to

force Mary Allen into my version of a Christian wife was having in her life. We were drifting further and further apart. Although things looked happy on the surface, we both knew that our marriage was bruised and broken on the inside where the world could not see. Finally one night I said to her, "Honey, I can't deny the tremendous things which have happened to me these past two years because of trying to give my future to the finding of God's will. But I've been wrong in trying to force all this on you. No one forced it on me. I'm sorry I tried (however unconsciously) to manipulate you by taking you to all these meetings etc. to get you converted. I am really sorry." I went on to tell her, "When we got married I didn't sign up to *change* you, just to *love* you . . . and I do, just as you are."

This took the pressure off her, because I really meant it. Within a few weeks she went out and made a beginning commitment of her future to Christ all by herself, in the way which was right for her. (And it almost hurt my feelings that it didn't happen through me, but through a friend.) Now I can see how wrong I've been so many times in these past few years in trying to change people instead of loving them. I believe we delude ourselves in thinking we can change people anyway. I am convinced that only God can convert anyone.

What happens when God's will becomes personally real and important to both partners in a Christian marriage? Then for the first time a Christian home is a live option. Now in the soul of our marriage it was not *my* vision of what a marriage or husband should be against *her* vision—one of us always having to be wrong. But now, together we began trying to find out Christ's vision of what our marriage should be.

I found that in a Christian home the husband was to be the spiritual head (1 Cor. 11:3). This implied making some decisions which I had never made. The wife is to look to the husband for strength and authority under God (Eph. 5:22 f.). Because of my insecurity I had been straining so hard to make our home a democracy that she had never really been able to look to me for these things. But now that we both wanted a Christian home we began to try to live together in a new way. The awful sniping at each other wasn't necessary to gain supremacy points or get even. We could afford to admit more often that we were wrong and help and accept each other with all of our faults, because we began to feel deeply accepted by God, even though we were seeing our selfishness more and more as we looked toward Christ.

For the first five years of our marriage I had been trying somehow to prove to my own wife that I was a "man"; and finally I could admit (she already knew of course) that I am only a little boy trying to impress the world that I am a man. Then we began to be able to tentatively relax and sometimes be children in the soul of our marriage and find peace together.

All of this does not imply that a Christian marriage is one with no problems or even a marriage with fewer problems.

(It may well mean *more* problems.) But it does mean a life in which two people may become more able to accept each other and love each other in the *midst* of problems and fears. It means a marriage in which selfish people can sometimes accept selfish people without constantly trying to change them—and even accept themselves, because they realize personally that they have been accepted by Christ . . . by God. And they are involved together in the adventure of trying to find God's will for their lives. And there are no guarantees that they will work out all their problems.

In honesty I must say that I am still an egoist and still a coward; but now, because of God's amazing gift of His presence and the perception which comes through beginning to give one's life to Him, I can sometimes live and make decisions in my own personal life as if I were not these things. And believe me that is Good News!

CHAPTER
FIVE

Thy will be done,
  On earth as it is in heaven.

Matthew 6:10, RSV

A
LIFE
WITH
PRAYER

W<small>HEN I WAS A SMALL BOY WE LIVED</small> in a two-story house near the edge of town. One day I was playing alone in my parents' bedroom upstairs. I was sitting on the floor, completely absorbed, playing with some toy soldiers, a brass tray, and a large battered tablespoon, among other things. Suddenly I looked up and realized I was totally alone in the house. I remember the throbbing silence. The aloneness terrified me and I began to sing and beat on the brass tray with the battered tablespoon, somehow feeling that if I could only keep up the noise nothing would creep up and get me. I remember being afraid to shout "Mother" for fear it (whatever it was that was going to get me) might know I was frightened and come out of its hiding place. The terror was agony; and I remember singing at the top of my lungs and beating the brass tray with huge tears streaming down my face and my heart about to jump out of my chest. When at last my mother came in from the backyard and came upstairs, I can still remember the feeling of exhaustion and the tears of relief as I collapsed into her arms and was released from my self-made prison of noise and fear.

I think something that "felt" like this took place in that first attempt to surrender my will to God by the roadside. But it was *more* than emotion. Martin Buber has tried to describe what happens to a person when he or she encounters God personally. He says, "Man receives and he receives not a 'specific content' but a Presence, a Presence as power."[1] One is bound up in a new relationship. Now this is no lightheaded release from the responsibility of intelligent thought "nor does it in any way lighten his life—it makes his life heavier, but heavy with meaning. . . . There is the inexpressible conformation of meaning. Meaning is assured. Nothing can any longer be meaningless. The question about the meaning of life is no longer there. But were it there, it would not have to be answered. You do not know how to exhibit and define the meaning of life, you have no formula nor picture for it, and yet it has more certitude for

[1] Martin Buber, *I and Thou* (New York: Charles Scribner's Sons, 1958), p. 110.

you than the perception of your senses."[2] This was true for me as I set out to try to live my life for Jesus Christ.

But one of the first things I came to realize was that I didn't know how to begin to find God's will for me particularly. I had always rather naïvely assumed that the making of a "total commitment" sort of automatically ushered into one's experience a vital prayer life (whatever that meant) and ushered out the preoccupation with old resentments, fears, or fantasies of sleeping with someone other than one's wife.

I have always pictured my inner life as a sort of cavern inside my head out of which I look at you, the rest of the world, through my eyes in the wall of the cavern. This cavern has a pool of liquid filling it about two-thirds full. The part above the surface of the pool is my conscious life and the larger part, beneath the surface where I cannot see, is my unconscious life. The day I decided to commit my life wholly to God, I scooped up everything I could see above the level of consciousness and offered it to Christ. I felt free; but then, several mornings later a hoary head came up out of the slimy pool, an old resentment.

I was filled with discouragement and I thought I must not have really committed my life to God at all. But then I realized joyously that of course I had—that all a person does when he commits his "whole life" is to commit that of which he or she is conscious. And according to many psy-

---

[2] Ibid.

chologists, the major part of the human psyche is below the level of consciousness.[3] So the totally "committed" Christian life is a life of continually committing one's self and problems day by day as they are slowly revealed to his or her own consciousness. I think many Christians have become discouraged or given up because they have at some time made a new beginning with God and then found their minds filled with guilt, resentment, and jealousy. Discouraged, they have assumed that they are not in right relationship with God at all. Naturally they do not want to admit these problems in their Sunday school classes, since they assume the rest of us are not plagued with such horrible and unchristian thoughts.

But since I now wanted to commit my future to God, I had to find out *specific* ways to align my rebellious and wavering will to His. I had always "prayed" sporadically; but my prayer life was a rather mechanical monologue. I had prayed about *big* things (cancer, success, deliverance) but didn't want to disturb God over the *little* problems of everyday living (resentment, jealousy, slothfulness). Now suddenly I realized that there are no small decisions—since every deciding either takes one closer to or further from God's will.

In order to develop a fulfilling prayer life, I had tried books of prayer, reading Psalms and all sorts of devotional

---

[3] See Jolande Jacobi's *The Psychology of C. G. Jung* (New Haven: Yale University Press, 1962), pp. 5 f.

books. But again and again I wound up praying something like: "Dear God, forgive me for all the bad things I do. Help me to be better; thank you for all the many blessings you have given me; and help everybody everywhere." That prayer seemed to pretty well cover everything, but nothing much *happened* in my life. Then people began to tell me I needed to have a certain period of time each day for private prayer. I tried that . . . and failed, again and again, to get up that few minutes before everyone else did in the mornings.

I can remember the alarm going off those mornings (very early). I would wake up and force myself to my feet to feel around in the dark for my robe and slippers in the closet or for my Bible in the blackness. If I couldn't find everything right away, I would tell God sleepily, "Lord, you know it is not fair for me to wake up my family (who need their sleep) just to satisfy my selfish desire to have a time of prayer. Deliver me from that kind of legalism." And I'd go back to bed.

Or I can remember waking up early on cold winter mornings after a late night up and saying, "Lord, you know how unreasonable I am with my family when I don't get enough sleep. And since you have made it clear to me recently that I should be more thoughtful of them, I'm going to sleep this morning . . . knowing . . . you will . . . understand."

Or I can remember other times when I have awakened and decided to pray in bed in that semi-drowsy, half-conscious state (when the will is disengaged). These times certainly felt "spiritual," but they are not, I learned, to be confused with conscious Christian prayer.

Nothing seemed to be working and I knew there was something really missing in my prayer life. Finally one day I met a layman whose life had a power and a concern in it which I knew instinctively were the things my Christian life desperately lacked. Everywhere this man went he left in his wake business men and women who began to be different people and whose lives became disciplined and focused on the Living God. I asked this man what he considered to be most important in the discipline of his Christian life. He pointed out that reading the Scriptures every day and having a specific time of prayer for the cultivation of a real and dynamic relationship with Christ were the two things which had become most meaningful and real to him.

Seeing a *life* with which I could identify did for me what all my "trying" could not—motivated me to begin a regular time of prayer and devotional reading of the Bible each day. I began, and through faith in another man's faith, was able to continue through the dry periods until this time became the center from which I live the rest of my life.

At this point things began to change. I realized that if Christianity is a living relationship with God I had to find out what this God is really like to whom I had committed my future. I realized that my closest relationships had always been with those who knew the most about me, and loved me anyway. So I began to reveal my inner life to

Him, all of it (even though I knew He already knew). This experience taught me the strange power in prayer of being *specific* with God. After making as total and complete a confession of all of the moral weaknesses and specific sins I could recall, I thanked Him for His forgiveness. I began to examine myself daily and "keep current accounts with God."

In trying to be totally honest I found a new freedom and sense of being accepted. Now I didn't psychologically need to gloss over my true greed and lust and excuse it as being insignificant. I knew I was accepted. Instead of saying, "Lord, today I exaggerated a little on my expense account, but you know everyone does," I was able to say, "Lord, I *cheated* on my expense account today. Help me not to be a dirty thief." Or instead of saying, "Lord, I exaggerated when I described that business deal," I began to be able to level with God and simply say, "Lord, I lied again, trying to make myself feel more important. This is the kind of man I am. Forgive me and give me the power and the desire to be different."

As I read passages like 1 John 1:9[4] I began to really believe that God could forgive me and would. And the pressures inside my life began to change. Things began to be different not only in my devotional time but in my whole day. In looking for *specific* things to thank God for each

---

[4] "If we confess our sins, he is faithful and just to forgive us our sins, and to cleanse us from all unrighteousness" (KJV).

morning I began to see His hand everywhere, and life became richer and filled with good things.

For a long time I had been disturbed about the problem of a wandering mind during my time of prayer. I would be trying to pray and suddenly my mind would jump to a business appointment I needed to make. For years I had forced these thoughts out of my mind to get back to "spiritual things." But now, thanks to another Christian friend, I began to keep a list by my side; and when the thought came to me to call someone, to make an appointment, or to do something for the family, I began to jot it down and then go back to God. I was at last realizing that He is interested in my total life and that these things which came into my mind during my time of prayer might be significant things for me to do, or places for me to go. This also made it easier for me to get my mind immediately back to my other prayers.

Sometimes a vision of someone I resented would come floating into my prayers or some incongruous situation that I did not want to think about. Instead of suppressing it, I began to offer the person or the thing immediately to God in prayer, asking Him to make my thoughts about this person more like His. I began to keep a list of people for whom I wanted to pray. And before I knew it, I discovered that God was touching more and more of my life through this time of prayer. I realized experimentally that the Incarnation means that God has made the material world of people and things His concern and that we must make it our concern for Him.

But there was a fly in the ointment. I found that although I had believed God could forgive me for all my selfishness and sins, I discovered that I could not forgive myself for one of them in particular. After months of inner anguish and continued confession I was talking to a close Christian friend. In a prayer I confessed this sin aloud to God before this friend. And within a few days, I could accept God's forgiveness. As a Protestant I had always been repelled (and frightened) at the idea of revealing my true self before another person. But now I realize why Luther made the admonition in James to "confess your sins to one another" (5:16) a part of the priesthood of all believers. [5]

This experience opened a whole area of my Christian life. I realized that once we have confessed our most awful sins to God *before another person*, we can never again pretend (comfortably) that we are righteous . . . however famous we may become as Christians. We can quit wasting so much of our energy explaining ourselves and making sure that everyone understands that we are good people. Because now we know that at least one other fallible human being knows that we are not. We are selfish sinners. I am not necessarily recommending this to anyone. I am merely saying that *I* was trapped with some terrible anguish; and through this kind of specific confessing with a trusted friend (whom I knew might fail me), I found myself in a position in which I had to trust God with my reputation . . . and I

---

[5] Martin Luther, *Works*, V/36, p. 86.

found a new freedom. I could begin to be more my true self with other people, realizing that as awful as I am, Christ loved me enough to die for me and people like me. Now I really *wanted* to be different in my life *out of gratitude*.

At this point a new honesty crept into my prayers. Before this, I had always started out by saying, "God, I adore You" (whether I really did or not that morning). Now I could say (when it was true), "Lord, I am sorry, but I am tired of You today. I am tired of trying to do Your will all the time, and I'd like to run away and raise hell." But now I could also continue, "But, Lord, forgive me for this willfulness: and even though I don't 'feel like' it, I ask You to lead me today to be Your person and to do Your will." This was a real act of *faith*, because there was no religious feeling involved. My days began to take on the character of adventure.

Howard Butt, Jr., has been a tremendous help to me at this point. He once told me about waking up one morning and beginning a time of prayer only to find that he was as stale and flat as he could be. He couldn't sense God's presence at all. But he said, "God, I thank You for being with me even though I don't *feel* as if You are within a thousand miles." When he said this, I at once thought it sounded like some kind of autosuggestion; but he continued and said, "Lord, I believe You are here, not because I feel like it, but I believe it on faith in the authority of Your Word. You said You would be with us." As he continued, I realized that in so much of my life I had been a spiritual sensualist, always wanting to *feel* God's presence in my prayers and being depressed when I didn't. I saw that until I could believe *without* spiritual goose pimples I would always be vacillating, and my faith would be at the mercy of my emotional feelings. So I tried this praying whether I felt spiritual or not; and for the first time in my life found that we *can* live on raw faith. I found that often the very act of praying this way brings later a closer sense of God's Presence. And I realized a strange thing: that if a person in his praying has the *feeling*, he doesn't really need the *faith*. I began to feel very tender toward God on those mornings during which I would pray without any conscious sense of His Presence. I felt this way because at last I was giving back to Him the gift of faith.

Things began to change more rapidly in my inner life. It wasn't that I got rid of all my problems (as many Christian witnesses and evangelists seem to imply, thus making us feel guilty and inadequate when we have problems). But I simply began getting a *new set* of problems. I came to realize that God wasn't going to take things out of my life. Instead He *brought in* a great many positive new things. Since my life and my time were already filled to overflowing, some things had to go . . . but He made *me* choose what they would be. And it was a great day when I found my whole set of values and my honest secret inner desires were changing. In a life of faith, I discovered, "renunciation is not sacrifice."[6] I had read and now saw the truth in the late Ma-

[6] Louis Fischer, *Ghandi, His Life and Message for the World* (New York: Mentor Books, 1960), p. 34.

hatma Gandhi's statement: "Only give up a thing when you want some other condition so much that the thing has no longer any attraction for you, *or* when it seems to interfere with that which is more greatly desired."[7] At first I had thought that if this were true I was stuck with some of my problems for life. But now I found that this advice was actually becoming true in my own prayer life. I began to *want* to be Christ's person enough to pray that He would reveal to me those thoughts and habits which were standing between Him and me and my doing His will. I prayed that He would then give me the desire and the power to change.

Right here I ran into a problem that is very subtle even among the ranks of the newly committed disciples of our Lord. The problem was this: for years I had been engaged in a conformity to the social and economic world. This conformity had influenced the kind of clothes I wore and the kind of house I lived in, etc. But now, having recognized this conformity to the world, I was tempted to trade it (unconsciously) for a conformity with the prevailing opinions of my new Christian friends concerning my behavior. In other words, as I prayed that God would reveal any changes I should make in my life, I was at the same time being pressured from the outside to make changes by Christian friends who were slightly appalled at some of my activities as a "good Christian." I am convinced that the changing of

---

[7] Ibid. See Christian expression of this experience reflected in the fourteenth chapter of Romans.

your behavior as a Christian for *any* reason other than that of honestly believing that *Christ* would have you change it leaves the door open to all kinds of cliquish spiritual pride and self-righteousness (regardless of whether or not the change itself is good).

But how does one actually go about deciding to change his social and ethical behavior as a committed Christian? And, having decided, how does one carry out these changes without being a pious fraud? Several years ago I might have thought that these questions were out of place in a discussion on a life of prayer. But if a Christian life is one of praise and adoration and the conforming of one's life and the world around him to the purposes and will of God, then I realized that a life of prayer, to have any fiber or reality about it, had better also deal with the areas yet unchanged.

One of the things God brought into my already full life as a young business man was the desire to tell other people that life wasn't a hopeless rat race, to tell them the Good News. This led to my beginning to teach an adult Sunday school class. Because many of the members of this class were college professors with advanced degrees, my intense pride demanded a great deal of study and preparation for Sunday morning. As I began to study about ten hours a week for my thirty-minute talk on Sunday morning, several things began to demand change.

We had often stayed out late on Saturday nights, going to dinners, movies, dances . . . mostly involving some preparatory social drinking, some sustaining social drinking and/or some later "one for the road" social drinking. But as I began to go home and try to put the finishing touches on my Sunday school lesson at 2:30 A.M. some Sunday mornings, I realized that just as a practical matter if nothing else, some changes were in order. So we started coming in earlier. When we began to reserve Sunday as a family day with the children, we found that we felt terrible physically after a late evening with too much to eat or drink. I discovered that in order to be a loving parent and thoughtful husband (which I now really wanted to be) I needed more sleep than I was getting anyway. So I began to *want* to live a life with order and moderation in it enough to see how we could have one. And the subsequent changes in our social life opened a whole new world of personal relationships and family activities I had never before "had time for."

All this time, while I was praying for God to reveal His will to me, I was being confronted in my soul with relationships which needed changing, attitudes toward my family, my work, sex, the magazines I was reading, my lack of involvement in politics as a Christian, and a good many other things which brought me to my knees continually in frustration mixed with the joy of knowing that God was changing my perspective and and desires. He was giving me the power to occasionally be the free man I had always wanted to be in these areas.

As I continued to pray and read the New Testament, I learned that Christ's criteria for a godly life were not doctrinal as ours so often are. His had to do with allegiance to

Himself and the *fruits* that allegiance produced in a person's *relationships with other people* (John 1:12; Matt. 7:15 f; 11:2 f; 12:33; 25:31 f; Luke 10:29–37, etc.). And I began to see that a life of prayer is to be judged ultimately not so much by even our devotion in praying and witnessing and inner moral rectitude as by whether or not we have fed the hungry, clothed the naked, and loved the loveless stranger (Matt. 25:31 f.). It dawned on me with a sudden jolt that real prayer, Christian prayer, inevitably drives a person, sooner or later, out of the privacy of his or her soul, beyond the circle of his or her little group of Christian friends and *across the barriers between social, racial, and economic strata to find the wholeness, the real closeness of Christ in that involvement with the lives of His lost and groping children, whoever and wherever they may be.*

But behind and woven through all of these outer problems and adjustments had developed a new inner prayer life. There was a sense of active adventure. My prayers were no longer vague mystical "feelings." I was communicating with a God who was *alive,* about real issues and real people in my days and nights. God was trying to give me an abundant new experience of life, when and if I would take it . . . a day, an hour at a time. When my regular morning prayers would start out "dry," I learned to read devotional books (like *My Utmost for His Highest* by Oswald Chambers or *The Imitation of Christ* by Thomas à Kempis) to turn my thoughts toward Him, toward Christ. Then I had found that by following any such reading with a passage from the New

Testament every day I was gradually filling my unconscious life with God's message. And as I was revealing myself to Him in confession, He was revealing His character and purpose to me through the reading again of the way Christ reacted throughout the story of His life, death, and resurrection and of His Spirit in the formation and development of the early Church.

I began to see as I never had the relationship of my prayer life to my physical and emotional life. A large glass of hot water, a few minutes of regular exercise or jogging just before one's prayer time each morning can change the whole climate of one's relationship with God and with other people. Because we are to come to Him with our whole lives . . . not just our "spirit."

I have learned to love Christ personally. For now we have been through years of struggles and failures and joys together in the privacy of my soul and on the outer stage of my life. I have come to want to find new ways to praise Him for giving me forgiveness and His Spirit, and a sense of unity, of wholeness, in my life. All of the different personalities I had projected in the various areas of my experience were somehow beginning to be melded into one. I didn't have to have a separate vocabulary, a different kind of humor and a different set of ethics for my business life, my church life, my family life, and my prayer life. It was as if Christ had taken His fist and begun to knock out the partitions in my soul which had made my life so fragmented.

Finally, I began to see that prayer is not a series of requests to get God to help me do things I think need to be done. Prayer is a direction of life, a focusing of one's most personal and deepest attention Godward. The purpose is to love God and learn to know Him so well, that our wills, our actions will be more and more aligned with His, until even our unconscious reactions and purposes will have the mark of His love, His life about them. Prayer was no longer an "activity." It had become the continuing language of that relationship God designed to fulfill a human life. But about this time I found that I simply couldn't live it alone.

CHAPTER
SIX

. . . woe to him who is alone when he falls and has not another to lift him up.

Ecclesiastes 4:10, RSV

GROUPS
FOR
STRUGGLERS

At this point in my pilgrimage I could identify with Christian in *Pilgrim's Progress* when he had seen the cross and had had the burden of his separation lifted from his life but was really only beginning his journey. I was experiencing a new kind of life. In perceiving the trap of my own self-centeredness I could also see others trapped in theirs and could begin to love them and want them to find the freedom I was beginning to find. I had begun to try to *hear* Mary Allen and the children and other people in my life, really listen to what they were saying. I had begun to look to see what their dreams and frustrations were as people. At church I had begun teaching a class with many apparently interested people in it. But here I was stymied. I knew God was real and knew He was doing miracles in my own home. But I was having a terrible time communicating the things I knew experientially to be true to other members of the church I attended. The people in the Sunday school class seemed to accept me and believe what I told them; but their lives were not changing. At least they were not changing in ways observable to me. I found that by myself I kept losing the perspective and the vision of Christ's purposes, and I was frustrated.

Out of my own loneliness and discouragement I decided to ask a few people to begin meeting with me one night a week for an eight weeks' trial period. My first inclination was to ask some of the "other" leaders of the church, my thinking being that if *they* would see this new life, the whole town might come alive. But to my surprise they were almost all too busy with meetings etc. to want to come. So I thought about Christ and what He did. Then I decided that I would look around the church and find eleven or twelve people who seemed most hungry to know God, whoever they might be. I found a couple who were dear friends who had just lost a child, a divorcee, a young man getting ready to go to seminary, a couple who had no children, a woman who had come into the Episcopal Church from the Roman Catholic Church recently, a man who sold heavy road equipment and one couple in the building business with four children. I went to see these people individually and told them what was happening in my life and asked them if they would like to meet with other people who were seeking to know Christ. The only criterion for joining the group was that each of the people had to *want* to give his life to God (even though he might not be able to do it).

The small groups in my past church experience had provided no answer per se; and many times they had degenerated into cliques, gossip sessions or debating societies. So this time we decided that the clear purpose was to be: getting to know the Living Christ. We were not going to argue about the *existence* of God, but were going to try to find out how each of us might get to *know* Him personally as He is revealed in Jesus Christ.

We decided to make an experiment with each one of our lives during that period and to report back to the group each week concerning our failures, our joys, and the ridiculous things which happened to us as we tried to take Christ consciously through the routine of our days and nights. We made it sort of a secretive thing . . . like an underground experiment. And we came back to each meeting with an excitement as we began to see how strangely timid and insecure we were in our faith. We could laugh at ourselves and vicariously experience through each other the fears and joys and insights of trying to live with Christ in the center of our lives.

We divided the time into three sections during those evenings. As we shared the problems and discoveries of each week we began to see together the fresh and contemporary footprints of Christ through our lives. We studied the

Bible. Most of the people never really had and admitted that they were ashamed of how little they knew about the content of the Bible. And we spent the last part of the evening praying together.

As those eight weeks grew into two years, and as we studied the Bible and shared our own real lives, we found that we had never really known each other at all before the group started. We found that we had not been able to communicate because we were basically afraid of each other somehow and did not know how to reveal our true selves without being embarrassed.

After about two years one of our ministers came to me (I had talked to him about the group prior to its beginning, which I strongly recommend doing) and asked me what I was telling the group about financial stewardship. I tried to think, and realized that we had never talked about giving, as such. The minister wondered because several of the people in the group had obviously begun to tithe and all of our personal giving to the church had increased considerably. I began to get excited as I realized what was happening to us as individuals apart from our time together each week. Several of the people had become church school teachers, one the superintendent of the Sunday school, one had become head of the Women of the Church and had so loved the group that she had been appointed area director of Episcopal Women's work for a large part of the state. Three of us had been elected to the vestry of the church. And all of us had found new life in our own church experience. Because now we had something to talk about. Christ was not a distant figure but through the Holy Spirit He was becoming alive in our midst. We felt a different kind of love for each other, for other people, and for Him. I realized that these were the things our vestries and Christian Education committees had been trying to make happen for years. We had found them to be only the *by-products* of getting to know the Living Christ together.

Now my own inner life had taken on a whole new dimension. I was not alone in it. The group became a spiritual family to come back to with my failures and successes. My whole concept of group leadership suddenly had taken a change. I can remember the strange paradox as "group leader" when the group finally came alive. In the beginning Mary Allen had been skeptical about having a regular gathering of people with different backgrounds in age, marital status, social habits and interests and hoping for any kind of common ground. But I felt that these were the people whom God had given us. And besides, if it failed nothing would be hurt but my pride. I wasn't selling anything; so we tried it.

Things went pretty smoothly until about the third meeting. To put us all on a more equal basis and to force us to examine the Scriptures for ourselves, no one was allowed to use the Bible commentaries until *after* a session in which the passage was discussed. This saved the people from the anxiety of expressing an honest opinion for fear the leader had *the* answer and was ready to pounce on them with it.

But about the third meeting, I expressed an opinion about

the meaning of the passage, and two of the members of the group heartily disagreed. A third took up their position. We checked the passage for study in the secondary sources for the next week, and the meeting ended. As it turned out they were right and I was wrong. I felt sick. I had been so sure that I was right. I felt that I had failed them as a leader and that they would lose confidence in me and the group would disintegrate. I told all this to Mary Allen and was reconciled to my failure. But during that week one member of the group after another called, filled with enthusiasm, telling me they thought that at last the group was coming alive and that *that* meeting had meant more to them than any of the others.

Right then two thoughts struck me: (1) That a Christian leader must die in a sense to his own image of perfection that others may live. Now the people realized I was just one of them and that they too were first class citizens and not just "my group." My being wrong and their being able to help me did something for all of us. I quit having the pressure to be right all of the time as leader and relaxed more. They gained a new kind of group confidence and freedom. (2) It hit me that when the group leader is in control and things "feel good" to him about a meeting, it is not necessarily good from the *participants'* perspective. Many times the leader's very painful experience of "laying down his life for his friends" in witnessing to his own failure and being vulnerable makes for an exciting and joyous breakthrough for the *rest* of the group. This seeing *them* come alive and gain confidence was paradoxically a far greater joy than having a "successful group" as a smooth leader. This was true even though my pride seemed to be taking all kinds of blows.

As the months had gone by and we had met in each other's homes to pray and talk about Jesus Christ, our homes became more natural places to talk about Him during other nights of the week. We began to learn vicariously through each other's experiences. One of us would tell the group: "I have a neighbor who has been mean to our children for years, and I've despised her. Now I find that we have been elected president and vice-president of the P.T.A. What can I do to let her know that I now love her? The two of us have a meeting set for tomorrow." Then someone else in the group who had recently faced resentment in his own life would witness to his own struggle; and out of this dialogue often concrete suggestions came to us which we might not have stumbled onto alone for years because of our lack of perspective, each being so close to his own problems.

As time went on I found that I desperately needed the balance, correction, and love of such a group. The openness and acceptance helped me more and more to be honest—not only with the group but in my business life and at home. The fresh witness of lives being changed before one's eyes brings a perpetual newness and wonder when your own experience gets flabby and gray.

I will never forget a young couple, whom I shall call

Betty and Joe, who were a part of a later group. One night Betty came into the group. She was very attractive and had three lovely small children; but she told us (later) that her marriage was on the ropes. She was a very vivacious swinger-looking type who flirted outrageously and delighted in telling shocking stories to mixed groups. She had been a churchgoer for years. But now, out of a deep need she came and gave herself as wholly to Christ as she knew how. And her life began to change in a marked way. I remember eight weeks later she was leading us in a period of prayer. Afterwards she said quietly to the group, "You know, all my life I've been trying to get your attention; I have showed off, told risqué stories, and done all kinds of things to get you to notice me, to love me." She paused and then continued, "And when you didn't, I gossiped about you, cut you to ribbons behind your backs, because I was miserable. I wanted to be something; I wanted so much to be something in your eyes. But now," and she stopped and looked very radiant and at peace as she continued, "for the first time in my life I'm happy to be nothing for Jesus Christ, just to be the mother of our children . . . and Joe's wife."

But almost immediately upon entering this new kind of life, Betty had asked us, "What am I going to do about Joe?" This was a question many people had been wondering for years. Joe was a winsome young man in his early thirties who was financially interested in the funeral business in that part of the state. He was also interested in gambling. And to give you an insight into his local reputation at that time, some of his friends called his largest funeral parlor "Joe's Place." We had told Betty to go home and be a different wife, to love Joe and quit trying to change him. Well, the next week Joe showed up at the meeting . . . very suspicious.

One night about sixteen weeks later, Joe led us in a period of devotion on the cross which was ruggedly beautiful. It was beautiful because it was filtered through a real life which was experiencing salvation. And it came to us clearly in our own language without the impediment of religious jargon. When he had finally finished he said to us, "You know, sixteen weeks ago I came out here to laugh at you, and to prove to Betty that whatever it was she had found I didn't need. But after I'd been here an hour, I knew that this was important. And after two hours I knew you had found what I'd been looking for all my life . . . in all the wrong places. I knew you had found the meaning of life."

What we were seeing in this group was God working in the "now," and I cannot describe the sense of joy and elation, the sense of discovery and belonging and being loved which almost miraculously developed in these meetings (which paradoxically dealt mainly with the *problems* of giving one's self and one's situation to God and to other people).

As these and later groups continued, we found that each time we had to face the danger of becoming an inbred little clique; and we would bring in new people in various ways. But we also began to realize that being a Christian meant more even than the ebb and flow of meeting together in our group on Thursday nights and for worship on Sundays and then going casually out into our separate lives as witnesses. I began to sense that the group was helping some of us to get beyond a vague general approach to our Christian lives in the world. We were beginning to be helped—each to find the particular form or shape of his own obedience away from the group. Two of the older ladies in one group felt impelled to visit the sick and learned to help them in practical ways. Two men were interested in integration and began to get involved in trying to see what they might do that would be both practical and truly Christlike. A doctor and a dentist began to approach their office routine and practices as they might have a foreign mission assignment. And the change in perspective changed both of their lives.

The couple I have called Betty and Joe felt led to change businesses, which entailed breaking lifelong ties and moving to another city at great financial risk. A doctor and his wife in a group in Indiana took a boy, a Cuban refugee, into their home to educate with their daughters while his parents were trapped in Cuba. The wife began visiting a young woman at the county jail and eventually got the woman released to their family's care to help her get a job and back on her feet. Another doctor and his family did the same thing for a nineteen-year-old boy in Corpus Christi, Texas. These things were not all easy, happy experiences. Yet even with the anguish and uncertainty of the changes and failures we and others were experiencing in these groups, we found a deep and solid joy, a real enjoyment of life in our close association in Christ.

But more important than our immediate enjoyment we found together that contemporary "Living Christianity" is not what we had thought it was at all. For us it became no longer a religion of sacred patterns of behavior and the study of solemn Reality. We found that it is actually not a "religion" at all, but *real* creative life, life in which we are free to be honest about ourselves and to accept and love each other and Him, because the Living Christ is in the midst of us . . . winning us to Himself and to His world. Suddenly we had something real to tell, something "which we have seen and heard!" Together!*

And then I saw my life as a business man from a new perspective . . . and was very disappointed.

---

* Editor's Note: Keith Miller and Bruce Larson have developed a series of thirteen-week group experiments for people wanting to start a group like that described here. *The Edge of Adventure* can be purchased from Villa Publishing, 6105 Mountain Villa Circle, Austin, Texas 78731.

CHAPTER
SEVEN

. . . no one of us lives, and equally no one of us dies, for himself alone.

Romans 14:7, NEB

GOD
AND A
BUSINESS
OFFICE

IT HAS NEVER CEASED TO AMAZE ME that we Christians have developed a kind of selective vision which allows us to be deeply and sincerely involved in worship and church activities and yet almost totally pagan in the day-in, day-out guts of our business lives . . . and never realize it. I came to see the appalling extent to which this can be true when, after having done four terms of seminary work, served on the vestries of two churches, and taught a large Sunday school class, a man who had worked in the same (oil company) division office I had for over a year said one day, "Gee, Keith, I didn't know you were a Christian." This stunned me into realizing that although I

had taken Christ by the hand and walked with [led] Him
through one passage after another in the labyrinth of my
soul, I had always left Him at the parking lot when I drove
in to go to my office.

I prayed about this but couldn't imagine how *I* could
witness for Christ in that particular situation. It wasn't that
it was so awful. It was just that the language, the risqué
stories, and the competitive atmosphere left no oxygen for
the spoken gospel to live in. Besides, I had been pretty fast
for years with little suggestive innuendoes and an occasional
profane outburst. Sigmund Freud has said, very percep-
tively I think, in his *General Introduction to Psychoanalysis*,
that these unchanged areas in our lives are like nature parks
which the city fathers in large metropolitan areas fence off
and allow to grow wild just as they always have, so the
citizens will have a little piece of the old life to wander
through to remember how it used to be.

I think this is what I had done with certain areas in my
outward life. Certainly I had done so with areas of my
inward thoughts, which I had walled off from the encroach-
ment of the Holy Spirit so that I might leave them just as
they always have been. This being the case with me, how
was I, of all people, supposed to bring the Living God into
my vocational situation?

But I could get no peace in my prayer time until I tried.
One morning I arrived at work, went into my private office,
and closed the door. I sat down and prayed that God would
somehow let me witness for Him that day. Within an hour

I had chickened out and was my same old attention-getting self. I was very discouraged.

At this point I stopped. Since I wanted to be Christ's person, yet didn't feel that I could effectively (or perhaps safely) do it in this pagan atmosphere, I thought this must be a call to go back to seminary and become a minister. Frankly, it would have been simpler in many ways, since people *expect* a minister to talk about Christ. But because of family and financial obligations, an investigation seemed to reveal that further education was out of the question. Intensely disappointed, I sat in my office one day and consciously surrendered my vocational life to Christ. As I sat there alone, it was as if my eyes were opened for the first time to the situation as it really was. I realized that the stereotype of the Christian minister I had carried in my mind all of my life had blinded me to the fact that God might want me to be His special representative in that office.

But I realized that I really didn't know how to "witness in my vocation." I guess I was afraid it meant getting a basket of tracts as some men do and wandering down the halls making people wish I would get fired so that they wouldn't have to dodge me and my Christian witnessing. This method had never seemed very effective when aimed at me in the past. As a matter of fact, now that I was a Christian I hated to be identified with those people (many of whom I knew were fine Christians). It wasn't that what they *said* was wrong; but there seemed to be a cool superiority about their attitude toward us sinners that didn't smack of the love of Christ. I was convinced that the God who had touched my life had loved me *before* I came to Him, just as I was in all my weakness. There had to be a different way for me.

But there was no trail to follow in this mission field filled with sharp sophisticated young men and women. I did not know even how to begin. To be honest, I was very reticent even to mention Christ's name to most of my associates. After several periods of frustration and procrastination, I decided to take Christ's Presence with me in my conscious mind clear through a day at the office. And this was the beginning. I soon learned that years of contrary thought patterns made it difficult to practice the Presence of Christ between concentrating on business matters. I was convinced that the quality of my work would be an integral part of any Christian witness I might have, so concentration on work was even more necessary. I realized that rather than worry about thinking of Christ all day, a Christian business person must commit the outcome of a piece of work to God and then really concentrate on the work.

To remind myself of God's presence I decided to pray every time I walked to and from the drinking fountain in the hall. Things began to happen. As I walked through the offices and spoke to people, I was praying; and I began to pray for *them*. Although I could not notice any outward difference in my own attitude, some of the love and concern I began to feel for these people must have communicated itself to them, because without my saying anything about my new intention in that situation, people began to come into my private office and talk to me about their inner lives. I soon realized that behind the smooth sophisticated faces in that company were many frustrated, lonely, and often frightened "little boys and girls" reaching out from the darkness of their souls for some meaning, some purpose in life. I began to see the extent of the need for Christ in the lives of "successful" people.

Before long I went to work for another company which was growing at a rapid rate. Another member of the management team there was a concerned Christian, but he, too, was stumped by the problems involved in trying to bring Christ consciously and effectively into a dynamic, hard-hitting, and very competitive business situation. We prayed together about it.

One Friday, when the executive vice-president was on a trip around the world and the pressures began to build due to critical business growth, I called my secretary into my office. "Lottie," I said, "I need to pray about this business. Monday morning I am going to come to work a few minutes early and pray in the conference room. If anyone else would like to do this too, they can."

I then went around to the department heads and secretaries and told them the same thing. This sounds very easy as I write it, but it was one of the most difficult things I had ever done in business. That weekend I kicked myself clear around the yard as I mowed it. Now, I had gone too far. It wasn't *my* company; and besides when no one showed up on Monday morning I would lose face as a manager. But I told God I was sorry for my lack of faith, confessed my self-centeredness, and said I was willing to fail for Him . . . I thought.

The next Monday morning almost all of the fourteen people in that office were in the conference room. I realized then that many people really want God to be a part of their vocational lives, but there is no feasible corporate trail to follow. We decided that if God is real enough to be in Christ, there must be an intelligent way to allow Him to become part of the situation of which we were a part. If not, He was too small to be God. We decided to pray for each other and for the people who came into that office, and we asked Christ to come into that company's life through us if it were His will.

This group was made up of people of very diverse religious backgrounds. There were a Presbyterian, two Roman Catholics, an honest agnostic, several Baptists, an Episcopalian, and one man who was studying Buddhism. We began to know each other on a different level. I began to love some of the ones I had only passed in the halls before. One day the man whom I felt was an agnostic, particularly concerning the person of Christ, came rushing into my office right after lunch and flopped down in a chair, looking very pale. That morning we had been talking about the fact that the Christian life and faith in

Christ can only truly be grasped experientially, through a committing of one's life. This had been hard for this man to see. He had an excellent academic mind. His father was an outstanding professor in biology at a Big Ten University. The young man had received a degree in chemistry and a graduate degree in geology with excellent marks. This idea of the *faith* in Jesus Christ having to come *before* the understanding sounded like intellectual suicide to him.

Now he was sprawled in a chair across from my desk staring at the floor. Finally he looked up and said, "Do you know what just happened to me?"

When I said I didn't, he related this story: It seems that on the way back to the office from lunch he had been driving in a crowded section of the city. Several cars ahead of him, a young mother had gotten out of a parked automobile and stepped backward right in the path of a truck, which struck her down. It all happened so quickly as he was inching toward the place where the woman's body lay that all he could remember was seeing the look of terror on the three-year-old little girl's face as she stared down at her mother through the open car door. A policeman had rushed up from the corner and was waving traffic around the accident. As my friend drove by, the dying woman looked up at him sort of pleading . . . and then disappeared from his view as he was motioned ahead in the traffic.

The shock of this incident had made a profound impression on the man opposite me in the chair. It had shattered the shell of intellectual sophistication, he said, inside which he had been living. It had revealed to him starkly his mortality, and the truth that his real objections to committing his life to Christ were not intellectual at all. They were volitional. He simply didn't like the idea of giving up his will to God or anyone else. And upon realizing this, as he had driven on down the street, he had suddenly known existentially who he was and who God was. In the same moment he wanted deeply to respond to the Christ whose presence and love he now sensed in his own experience. Right there in the car he had consciously committed as much of himself as he could to as much of Christ as he could perceive. He prayed that God would come into his life and reveal Himself more completely.

Needless to say, this man's deep conversion, the subsequent newness of life, and sharing with him the thrill of new discovery had a profound effect on several of us. We realized that it had taken place in an atmosphere of love and acceptance over a period of months in the office.

I cannot say that what happened because of our meeting together made the company a lot of money. I cannot even say what the real effect on other people's lives was. I don't know. But the effect in my own was amazing. I saw that it was difficult for a man to swear at one he has just prayed with. I saw that the women in an office have a feeling of being a real part of a living company of people when they have prayed with the men for the direction of their mutually shared vocational life. People began to treat each other more like people. This was true even though everyone was having to work under unusually heavy pressure at that time.

Men began to come in our offices, sit down and say, "What kind of a deal is this—these people laugh as if they were really happy." Together we began to learn to witness, to pray, to communicate what was happening in our lives to our wives, families and our ministers, learning to adjust to the problems of office situations as *Christian* business men and women. We had small groups of men coming to our offices to meet once a week to discuss the problems we faced in trying to be God's people in business. We would have sandwiches and discuss the Bible and its authority and relatedness to the new challenges we now saw all around us.

As we struggled with our own problems and those of the Christians whom we knew in the business community, we found that it is not easy to take Christ into one's business as Lord. If we are serious, we soon realize that we must work harder than our non-Christian competitors and do a better job at our business, because we must give up the "leverage" of cutting corners (in the inevitable dishonest practices in business and taxation procedures today). This may cost some money . . . a great deal of money.

People misunderstand your message. We found with Whitehead that, "the success of language in conveying information is vastly overrated especially in learned circles. Not only is language highly elliptical, but also nothing can

supply the defect of first-hand experience."[1] We came to realize that in the long run in our vocation the only real witness
which would last was not what we *said* about our beliefs but
what people saw us to *be*, week after week, in our dealings
with our associates and our competitors. This was not a glam-
orous witness, and we made many serious mistakes. We were
horrified as we began to see our real business personalities
revealed. We were honestly astonished at our continuing
selfishness and greed. Often we could only see our failure to
witness. But with all of the difficulties, we found that we were
experiencing the greatest life we had ever known. We saw the
lives of some intelligent, seeking people in our vocational
world changing before our eyes. Although we failed in many
ways, we found ourselves a part of a Purpose, a Challenge
which transcended the oil business.

Gradually we discovered a new sense of freedom from the
terrible responsibility to be successful in business *or* in
spreading the gospel. The *outcome*, we realized, was God's
business. Ours was to do the "specifics" before us that day.
Life began to be a different experience. We did not need to
pressure anyone to accept God's gift of Himself. The "inner
tracking" and actual converting could only be done by the
Holy Spirit. At last I understood what Barth meant when he
said about the Message: "I am glad I did not invent it, and
hence it is not my responsibility to defend it. My only task

---

[1] Alfred North Whitehead, *Adventures of Ideas* (New York:
Mentor Books, 1933), p. 286.

and privilege is to tell you that God Himself said so and says so until this day."[2]

We discovered that it was fun (though painful) to try to be honest with one's self. We found that it was appalling to discover the extent to which we deceived ourselves in our vocational lives. We found it crushing to be misunderstood as Christians. But transcending all these things, there was an inexpressible joy in sharing the experience of a business person beginning a new life and of watching that person begin to live for God. But the real revelation I think we found in trying to take Christ with us into our business lives was that the further "out on a limb" we seemed to be going to try to be obedient to Christ's will as we could perceive it, the more *real* He became. This led to the realization that Christ does not promise the business person great material success in his vocation (though this may take place), but rather Christ brings the *inner security* which one seeks through great material success . . . and having found this, the burden of succeeding may be lifted. And this inner security is discovered in the day-by-day relationship with Him.

What might happen to other people or groups of people who try to make their vocations Christian vocations? I do not know; but I think Dietrich Bonhoeffer came close to the answer when he said, "And if we answer the call to disci-

---

[2] Karl Barth, *Deliverance to the Captives* (Harper and Brothers, 1961).

pleship, where will it lead us? What decisions and partings will it demand? To answer these questions we shall have to go to Him, for only He knows the answer. Only Jesus Christ who bids us follow Him, knows the journey's end. But we do know that it will be a road of boundless mercy. Discipleship means joy."[3]

---

[3] Dietrich Bonhoeffer, *The Cost of Discipleship* (New York: Macmillan, 1961), p. 32.

CHAPTER EIGHT

. . . be doers of the word, and not hearers only, deceiving yourselves.

James 1:22, RSV

SHARING
THE
NEW
WINE

As I BEGAN SERIOUSLY TO TRY TO discover a way to articulate something of the reality I was finding in my own experience, I realized almost immediately that "saying words" is not what is meant by communicating the Reality of Jesus Christ. I think this is true regardless of how theologically correct the words may be.

In my reaction against legalistic, verbal religious "scalp gathering," I had for years decided that I would *live* my faith instead of *talk* about it. Now, I saw how totally selfish this "live the faith and not talk about it" idea is. It reminds me of a man in a dread disease ward marvelously meeting the doctor who had perfected a cure. The patient, as he was being (secretly) cured, walked back and forth in the same ward sort of flexing his muscles as he moved beds around and variously helped the other patients *die more comfortably*. His display of new wholeness only led the other patients to envy *him* . . . leaving their own deep illness unattended to. I saw that this patient had to somehow *introduce his dying fellows to the physician* so that they too could begin to be healed from their loneliness and incompleteness. I realized that I was this patient. This introduction to Christ, I saw, would take some *words* of direction.

As I began to ask outstanding church leaders how one person might tell another about the realness of God, I found that this business of effectively communicating Christian reality, of "witnessing," is probably one of the least understood areas of Christian living today, particularly among educated people. Everyone I went to beat around the bush. They simply did not know how to do this without being pious or obscure. I decided to try to see for myself what true effectiveness in sharing the Christian message and life might include. Immediately I was stumped.

Who can properly judge his own true effectiveness in other people's lives? For years, when things went wrong around our house I would try to "make things right" by bringing Mary Allen a present. But even if the surprise were a good one, it never seemed to strike a really deep chord of response. I sensed that she was somehow disappointed, though she managed to hide it well.

On the other hand, I can remember a particularly cold

and snowy winter night in Indiana. It was after supper. The wind was howling outside and we felt very cozy. Mary Allen was doing some sewing in one corner, and I was trying to read the newspaper on the sofa across the room. Our three little girls were giggling and climbing all over me as if I were a ladder. Finally I stopped trying to read and began to wrestle with them and love them. Through the tangle of little arms and legs I happened to see Mary Allen across the room . . . with tears of happiness streaming down her face.

I began to see that I, and the people I know, are most winsome in all our intimate relationships when we are unconsciously *being ourselves* with other people and accepting them just as they are, *without trying to manipulate or change them in any way*. But the very lack of self-consciousness that is so attractive makes those things we do at such times most difficult to analyze.

A minister often thinks he is most effective for God in the pulpit on that Sunday morning when he is preaching an eloquent sermon after hours of preparation. But between the nine and eleven o'clock services when he is in the process of going from one service to another—trying to relax a moment—someone urgently grabs his arm and says, "The superintendent of the children's department didn't come this morning!" So the minister has to go into the children's chapel and speak. He goes in and shares informally something of himself or the gospel message, never knowing as he rushes out to the next service that the mind of a little visitor on the back row was struck by his impromptu words . . .

and offered itself to God. Perhaps a great Christian life has been conceived . . . and the minister never knows.

I think a great deal of what happens deeply and positively to other people through our lives happens in this way. But, on the other hand, I found that there are a great many things we *can* learn consciously about sharing the newness of the Christian life and message. Most committed Christians have a great deal they could say about the reality and love of God, the relief of forgiveness, and the gift of purpose and relatedness to a life once filled with confusion and lack of meaning. Most of us have some things we might share in our business and social lives if only we knew how to go about it with real perception in the language we use for everyday living, so that we won't be hypocritical. The new groups of lay disciples in America are finding that one can sometimes get this message of salvation and a new life across. I want to discuss here specifically one way this can be done, or attempted, in the lives of people like many of us in the church today.

First of all I think there are at least three levels of communicating living Christianity; and most of the people with whom I had been acquainted only knew about the first level. For the great majority of churchgoing people, effective sharing of Christianity consists of studying the Bible and related books, speaking to lay groups about God, Sunday school teaching, preaching, living an ethical Christian life, being a good church participant, husband or wife, and worker at one's vocation, having an active concern for the important social and political issues of our time, and helping the poor. Most of us think a person who does all these things (layperson or minister) is really getting God's message across. Often such a man or woman develops quite a reputation as a speaker and Christian leader. But as important as this level of Christian sharing is, I have become convinced that it is only "contact work" for the Lord; and for years we have made it the whole enterprise. This type of Christian living and speaking often spreads a warm religious aura in a group; but it leaves few deeply and permanently changed lives in its wake. And without deeply changed and growing lives, there can be no "renewed church," no changed world, regardless of how full the churches are.

The second level of Christian sharing is that which is being reborn in the life of the church today. It is a person-to-person ministry, an actual conscious readiness on the part of an individual Christian to put another man or woman in touch with the Living God. This is not another "pat system" or "semi-canned sales pitch." It is rather a way of thinking about and being related to other people. It is an attitude based on the realization that behind the remarkably placid masks of the faces we see every day on the streets and in our businesses and clubs there lies a world of twisting souls, living with frustration and the fear of failure and meaninglessness, a world of souls without rudders, without any real sense of ultimate direction.

As I have implied earlier I think we in America may be

the "masters of deceit" in our personal lives. We have even deceived ourselves. We wear masks of success and happiness and integrity so much that we have even convinced ourselves that we are not such a bad people. Consequently we have not the basic prerequisite for coming to God . . . a conscious sense of Sin or separation from Him. Or at least so it would appear. Some theologians have made much of the lack of man's sense of Sin today. Reinhold Niebuhr spoke of "the universality of this easy conscience among moderns."[1] Although I think this generalization is far too broad, I do know that many people in our generation do not sense their basic separation from God (or Sin) as *guilt*. Today this separation often manifests itself in the vague indefinable anxiety, or the restlessness and incompleteness we have been discussing. So if one goes about trying to capitalize on people's conscious guilt to get them into a personal relation with God, he may miss many of the sharpest ones altogether and drive them away from Christ, since they simply don't experience their basic problem as guilt.

I have spoken to dozens of groups of all sizes and hundreds of individuals these past few years; and I have never

---

[1] Reinhold Niebuhr, *The Nature and Destiny of Man*, (New York: Charles Scribner's Sons, 1941), vol. 1, p. 94. See also D. M. Baillie, *God Was in Christ* (New York: Charles Scribner's Sons), pp. 162 f., for Baillie's view on modern man's lack of a sense of sin.

faced a group in which I was not convinced that many of the people were crying out in the privacy of their own hearts for some peace and direction in their souls. What I am saying is that there is a *very real need* for the life and message Christ brings; and this need is not far beneath the surface of modern life. This needs to be said since so many people are discouraged about sharing the Christian life when people look so self-sufficient all around them.

This is the way this kind of sharing might work. First, you find yourself in contact with another person, a natural, normal contact. Right here I think many Christians get off the track. I am so egotistical that when I became a Christian I was sure that I was sent to witness to the most outstanding group I knew (whom I considered my peers). But in reading the New Testament I was somewhat stunned to realize that even Jesus Christ evidently never made it in His own hometown, with His own local peer group (Mark 6:1 f.). And this did not seem to disturb nor deter Him in the least.

So I began to look around me at all the people whom God had already put in my life with whom I might develop a deeper and more personal relationship. I realized that without changing my daily routine one bit, I had a world filled with people, most of whom I had for years been ignoring. There was the man who sometimes helped me in the yard. There were the fellows in the gas station I traded with all the time, the parking lot attendants, the service people in the building my office was in, the waiters at the Petroleum Club, the secretaries, the bank tellers, and other men with whom I had coffee occasionally . . . and my own wife and children. As I began to see these people as *important people* who need God and His love, I realized that many of us active American churchmen are stumbling over the bodies of our wives and children and people in our daily paths to get out in the time-consuming, promoted evangelistic programs to find someone to love for Jesus Christ. I was later horrified to learn how subtly this temptation (to desert those closest to us in order to "do God's work") can come back again and again in different forms to erode our closest relationships.

As I began to read the New Testament accounts I saw that Christ almost never "went out of His way" to help anyone. He seems to have walked along and helped the people in His path. He was totally focused on doing God's will and going where God led Him. *But* He always seemed to help the people He met along the way while going where God directed Him. This made for an amazing steadiness and spiritual economy in His direction and ministry. This one change in my perspective made witnessing not a program but a *way of life.*

The second thing I realized was that we Christians have so cheapened the Christian message that most thinking people don't want any part of it. Our attitude betrays our lack of real faith. We act as if we were selling tickets to something, or memberships, instead of introducing people to Almighty God in an eternal and conscious relationship.

When a person buys a theater ticket he doesn't even have to think about it, it is such a casual transaction; and his attitude and verbal exchange with the ticket seller reflects this. But when you walk into a room in which two large corporations are about to consummate a merger, there is an air of gravity. Even a casual observer can tell that something important is taking place—because of the attitudes of the participants as they go about their business.

I think non-Christians do not read this kind of importance into our attitude when we are talking to them about Christianity. So I would say that in this kind of witnessing, we must think and pray in terms of a much larger God, a much greater and more transforming Gift of Life. I came to see that if people do not really believe we have found something that is terribly important to us, why should they want it?

After an outward personal contact has been made, then the *real* contact is made with the person behind the mask. I have found that this is done mostly by *listening* with real interest. What you are doing when you are listening as a Christian is putting your hand quietly in the other person's life and feeling gently along the rim of his or her soul until you come to a crack, some frustration, some problem or anguish you sense that person may or may not be totally conscious of. For example, let's assume you are talking to a man. As you are listening, you are loving this person and accepting him just as he is. The magic of this kind of concern is that you will often find your conversation moving imperceptibly from the general surface talk of the world situation and the weather into the intimate world of families and of hopes, of his life and yours. This change of climate sometimes takes place in a very short time in a listening atmosphere of concern and trust.

People today seem to be inwardly yearning for someone who really cares enough just to listen to them, without trying to change their reality. We don't even listen to each other this way in our own families very often. I am convinced that this fact is one of the key reasons for the tremendous amount of marital infidelity in this country. I do not believe that American men and women are possessed with an unnaturally strong sex drive. But having a lover, for instance, is having one who really knows a person's weakness and listens and accepts her anyway, just as she is.

But when one begins to listen honestly to people for Christ's sake with a word or look of encouragement, they often begin to cast out before you the shadows of a great number of the fears and uncertainties which are crouching just inside their hearts. Of course this account is greatly oversimplified for some relationships, but not for many (if you are really interested in the person).

In approaching life this way, do *not* think of the person you are listening to as a prospect for the church or as an object for your Christian witness. I know this may sound strange, but if you do think in these terms this will become a kind of spiritual manipulation. And instead of really listening you will be saying to yourself, "How can I get this conversation around to *spiritual* things?" Besides, from the other person's perspective your anxiety to get your "Christian content" across sends out the unspoken message that you have something more important on your mind (the person doesn't know what it is) than what he or she has to say.

So I began to merely listen to people with the idea in mind of making friends for Christ's sake. Soon I found that I could identify with almost every problem or sin I heard—if not with the deed, certainly with the emotion behind it. And this honest identification sometimes freed people to be their real selves. It became a bridge across which we could walk into each other's real lives. I found my life filled with a new and deeper kind of friendship than I had ever known before. But the point is that this kind of sharing begins not by spouting your *answer*, but by finding out who this person is and his or her problem, or need . . . *as that person sees it.*

In the Gospels I do not see Christ rushing up to people, grabbing them by the arm, and confronting them with a theological question. He seems to have walked down the road and listened to people describe their problems as they saw them. The people seemed to be so surprised and thrilled that someone saw their problems and took them seriously, that I rather imagine many responded totally and were made whole. And yet Christ knew these people's most basic problem was not withered hands or leprosy. But He met them where they were.

If and when your friendship with a man (for instance) grows, and it often will if you love him, and he acknowledges sometime that his life is not complete, *then* very naturally and simply you may want to tell him how you came to a realization in your life that it wasn't what it should be and how that realization caused you to turn to God. Tell your friend what God did; not to make you *good* (Christ was pretty clear about His attitude toward men claiming goodness; see Mark 10:18) but to make you *basically more joyful and hopeful.* And if you are not basically more hopeful *regardless of the many new problems you have as a Christian,* then you had better take a close look at your own relationship with Christ. You may have missed something very important in the gospel yourself.

When you have reached this point you will know whether or not this person is coolly detached or obviously seeking something in his own life. You know this because you have listened to him over a period of time and know his real interests and needs. But if after hearing about your life, he says something like, "Yes, uh . . . uh . . . say, did you hear what the Cowboys did yesterday?" don't panic, feel rejected, and say urgently, "What did I say to offend you?" or, "Don't you understand, friend, I'm about to lead you to salvation." But rather you might say something more like, "No, what did the Cowboys do?" and listen to him. He may only be backing off because you are getting too close to him.

Spiritually people are like fawns, ready to dart away at the first sign of what they consider any invasion of privacy. And since you are *not* selling anything, you do not have to be anxious. We Christians are the only people around who claim to have an eternal life; and yet in our urgency to *convince* people, we reflect nothing but anxiety and tenseness. But if this person has listened to your telling something about your own life and relationship to God and is interested, then you must, I believe, help him to see where *he* is now with regard to the gift of new life God is waiting to give him.

This is one way you can help him find out where he is in his relationship to Christ. Get him to look inside his own life, honestly. He doesn't have to tell you what he sees (this allows him to keep his privacy while considering what you are saying). Ask him to be specific with himself and with God. Let's say, so that you can see how it might feel to be talked to like this, that you and I are sitting across a luncheon table in a quiet place. We have known each other for some months and have come to the place in our relationship which I have just described. You have been an active churchgoer for years, but you are not experiencing this kind of newness in your adult Christian life which we have been discussing. You are really interested in knowing how you might make a new beginning in your own life. I will talk to you here as I would if we were together in the same room. If you are interested, then do the things I will ask you to do.

The first thing I would like for you to do is to look into your own inner life and ask yourself the question, "What is the most important thing in the world to me?" The temptation is to say, "God," but let me tell you some ways you can tell what is really most important to you. What do you think about again and again when your mind is not engaged with work or with someone else? Let me give you some suggestions of the kinds of things I mean: Do you think about a wife or husband (or children)? Do you think about being great in your vocation? Or being considered a brilliant person? Or socially sophisticated? Or are your recurring thoughts about sex or your own beauty? Or are your thoughts when alone centered in your own problems, jealousy, etc. . . . centered in yourself? When I ask myself this, some of the things I have come up with at various times in my life (if I am honest) are: thinking about myself as a successful athlete, business man, scholar, or writer. Or imagining or hoping people will think I am an extremely intelligent person. Or thinking about sex. Or at one time my thoughts were occupied with how I could become a great Christian minister.

Now each of these thoughts is like a rubber ball on a string tied to the center of your mind. You throw it out and get busy with the work of the day. But when you are alone, back it comes again and again to sit in the middle of the stage of your attention. I am asking you to consider this, because whatever you focus this hottest intensity of your mind on is very likely *what you worship instead of Christ!* For what is worship if it is not the object of your life's most intense focus?

I am not implying that Christ says that it is wrong to love one's children or wife or vocation. But it is dysfunctional to love them more than God. It is wrong to make idols of them. It ruins them and us. I believe that Christ intimates that we can never fully realize the gift of life which He came to bring us until we first know that we have loved ourselves and our way more than Him and His way (Matt. 9:10–13; Luke 15 and 18:18–30, etc.).

I have become convinced that the things which keep us from a live relationship to Christ are often not the "bad" things in our lives, but the good things which capture our imaginations and keep them from focusing on Jesus Christ.[2] I think this accounts for a good bit of our frustration as church members. We look around in our lives and say, "'No stealing, no murder, no adultery! Why, God, am I so miserable and frustrated in my Christian life?" But we have not seen the fact that we have never

---

[2] See discussion of this point in William Law's A *Serious Call to a Devout and Holy Life* (Philadelphia: The Westminster Press, 1955), chap. 7.

really offered Him the one thing He requires—our primary love.

What does one do when he finds out that he loves something more than God? For me it was rather terrifying, because the thing which was keeping me from the freedom of Christ was *my desire to be a great minister!* Because one's decisions will ultimately be made to conform with the shape of whatever has truly captured his imagination, my own decisions and sacrifices were not being made purely to love and feed Christ's sheep out of obedience and love of Him; but rather my decisions were made to help "the church's work" (*my* work) to its greatest fulfillment. This led to chaos and frustration.

When one sees, and can honestly face the fact, that his or her world is really centered in something besides God, in one's self in fact, I think that person faces the most profound crossroads in life (whether he or she is a layperson or a bishop). Because this is to recognize that one has separated himself or herself from God by taking God's place in the center of his or her own little world.

What does a person do? The answer is paradoxically the simplest and yet the most difficult thing I have ever done. In our age of complexity we want a complex answer, but Christ gives us instead a terribly *difficult* one. I think there are basically two things involved in coming to God as the center of one's life: (1) to tell God that we do *not* love Him most, and confess specifically what it is that we can not give up to Him; (2) to ask God to come into our conscious lives through His Spirit and show us how to live our lives for Him and His purposes . . . one day at a time.[3]

But what if you recognize that you *honestly do not* want God more than whatever is first in your life? I think this is where a good many perceptive Christians find themselves. In that case I would recommend that you (1) confess (as above) and then (2) tell Christ that your honest condition is that you cannot even *want* Him most. But tell Him that you *want to want* Him most (if you do), ask Him to come into your life at a deeper level than you have ever let Him before, and give Him permission to win you totally to Him-

---

[3] I am aware of the arguments of Buber and others against the position that once a person recognizes his idol as such, he can immediately turn the same kind of love on God. The Buber position points out (correctly, I think) that the love of idols is a possessive love, and that if we turn this same kind of love on God, we will blaspheme: "He who has been converted by this substitution of object now 'holds' a phantom that he calls God. But God, the eternal Presence, does not permit Himself to be *held*. Woe to the man so possessed that he thinks he possesses God" (*I and Thou*, p. 106).

Since I believe that kind of substitution of one's possessive love has led many evangelical Christians into a state of frustrated misery, I have here been careful to explain that the change I am referring to is from the possessive love of an idol to the *responding* love which is directed to the One we want to *possess us*, to guide us, to confront us at the core of our being with *His* Lordship and Life.

self. This may be your first honest encounter with Christ, and He will take you wherever you are. As a matter of fact, I believe this is really all *any* of us can do—give God *permission* to make us His. We certainly cannot be His by our own strength of will.

And if you made this new conscious beginning in a conversation with me, this is what I would tell you: that from now on you are not responsible to exert the pressure, to carry the burden of muscling yourself up to be "righteous." You are not *promising* to change, or to *have strength*, or to be a *great* Christian. You have only confessed your need and turned your life over to Christ. What a relief! If He wants me to change, He will furnish the motivating power by giving me the desire to change and then the strength to do it.[4]

But how does one begin living this new life every day? If a person makes this sort of new beginning in your presence, don't clap him or her on the back and walk off whistling. This is a terrifying experience to decide suddenly to give God your will, only to realize that you don't know what to

---

[4] This is not advising Christians to sit back and do nothing. It is rather a statement of the paradoxical fact that although good works are *inevitable* in the deeply committed Christian's life, I do not believe they are *required* to *establish* or *maintain* one's redeemed relationship. The relationship and the strength to live the life are gifts of grace.

do next. Christianity is not a *status* at which one arrives; it is a *life* in which one matures. So show this person the first steps one begins to take in this life with God.

Show him or her how to take a few minutes a day, *each* day, to begin developing this new relationship. Tell the person how to begin reading the Bible every day, and to begin to live and move into a new perspective. Tell him or her to look for the personality of God in all that he or she does and sees. Show the newly committed Christian how to get started at once in a vital sharing life with other strugglers. Take him or her into your own group and admit you are a struggler too. And if you don't have such a group in your own church, look for one or start one for your own sake. Explain to this person the discouragements that will come in actually trying to live one's life for God; describe the doubts; and point beyond them to the joys. Be honest, because there *are* doubts and discouragements; and unless such people know that *you* have them, they may doubt their own faith as the doubts hit them when they are all alone.

This kind of sharing of the Christian life and gospel produces more than attenders at church (though it almost always produces these). People who have seen themselves and accepted Christ as Lord and Master of their practical lives have not crossed the finish line of the Christian life; rather, for the first time they have climbed down out of the grandstand and gotten on the starting blocks as participants in that life in the *Living Body of Christ*.

So, as the first level of sharing Christianity is talking on

Christian subjects, church school teaching and Christian living, this second person-to-person level is the far more demanding business of living life, consciously loving person after person, listening to each one personally, privately, and then walking a few steps with each one toward the cross, and perhaps putting his or her hand quietly into the waiting hand of Christ . . . and His church.

CHAPTER NINE

. . . you put new wine into fresh skins; then both are pre-
served.

Matthew 9:17, NEB

WHAT
ABOUT
THE OLD
WINESKINS?

WHAT HAPPENS TO A MAN OR woman in modern American church life who suddenly finds a completely new orientation by making a serious beginning commitment to find and follow God's will? Paradoxically, many of us have found this sense of newness and deep engagement with life contrary to all our honest expectations as conscientious church attenders.

I remember one person with whom I prayed about such a new life several years ago. She had not been well for some time. When she opened her life deeply to God, she found that she could accept herself and her situation for the first time in years. Within a week she was off the sedation she had been told would be a part of her life from then on. She was radiant to see as she began struggling to learn to live with Christ in the center of things. I suggested that she tell her minister. She had been a loyal churchgoer for years, and it was natural to want to share her new discovery with her pastor. She went to him joyously. But his reaction was not one of joy. It was a grim and frowning response. She was urged not to get excited and be emotional. This would wear off and she should not do anything foolish. She was crushed. And if she had not had a small fellowship of people who accepted and loved her and allowed her to be freely joyful about God, she might have despaired and not found the tremendous and mature joy she subsequently has discovered.

Why did the minister react this way? This is not an isolated incident. This same scene has been repeated to my personal knowledge dozens of time during these past years. This growing body of new Christian disciples is constantly amazed at certain ministers' (often in their own denominations) rejection of them. This question must be faced if the new life being experienced by God's people is to be channeled through the existing structures of the institutional church.

So let's look at this problem briefly. First, from the *minister's* perspective what would an encounter like the one just described with one of his faithful parishioners look like? This minister had received his theological education at a large and academically respectable divinity school. He had been a professional minister for almost twenty years, a member of several important regional denominational committees (chairman of one), and had seen his parish grow in number of communicants and in size of financial budget rather substantially in the years since his ministry began. This man would be classified as a successful Christian minister.

But now this woman comes to see him who has been faithfully listening to his sermons for years. She says that all these years she has missed the whole point spiritually (under him). She implies (he thinks) that he didn't really tell her about Jesus Christ. Fortunately (he hears her to say), she has at last found the *real* truth of the gospel message; and finding the truth she has committed her life to Christ.

"How did you find out?" the minister asks.

"Why, through a friend, a layman."

"What is this layman's theological background?"

"Well, he has been in the oil exploration business for ten years. And he is a Christian."

In any case, she has found a new and joyous experience of life and wanted to share it with him. All this is shocking to the minister who has been preaching about the atonement and redemption for years. Her account sounds to a trained theological mind like the rankest kind of oversimplification . . . almost sawdust trail. He immediately suspects that this dear woman has been duped by some fanatic, and he is trying to think of some way to politely squelch all this before she gets badly hurt. He went through three years of tough postgraduate study, preached and exhorted for years, and now one of his key people comes to him spewing what sounds like nineteenth-century piety and implying (from *his* perspective) that *he* has missed the boat altogether. Not only that, but she is claiming to have found a kind of joy and new insight into her own life and into the meaning of the gospel which he knows is bound to be unreal . . . because he has never experienced it himself. And certainly he has sincerely wanted and prayed for whatever God has to offer His people.

But let's look at the same encounter from the point of view of the renewed Christian. After years of searching she has found in the past few weeks in her soul the meaning of life. God's forgiving love has suddenly become *real* to her. She loves Christ and His sinful people and realizes that she is truly one of them and is grossly self-centered. But she sees at the same time that she had been accepted and does not have to be the pious Pharisee any more. She has only to be loving and obedient to Christ's will as she can determine it, day by day. The burden of having to be a social leader is gone, and she can be herself at long last. She can adjust her priorities and her vocational career and help other people for Christ's sake. She has begun to become involved in doing this individually, through the church, and through social agencies aligned with her Lord's purposes. She has validated her experience in the pages of the New Testament (which before had seemed grossly exaggerated) and in the

living contemporary experiences of a small group of people
meeting weekly to find out who they really are and what
Christ and His purposes mean in our time.

So she goes to tell her minister about what is happening
to her, which she is sure he has been praying for for years.
But he is cold and, of all things (from her perspective), he
rejects her personally. She is trying to tell him that she has
seen her self-righteous behavior as a churchwoman, and at
last has begun to understand Christian love in a small group
of friends she meets with on Tuesday nights. But the minister only looks at her with a poorly disguised pained and
almost patronizing look (again from *her* perspective) and
tries to imply that all she has found is illusory and will soon
depart.

Now as this woman's experience deepened over the next
months and years (instead of disappearing), her relationship
with her minister and her confidence in him became increasingly difficult to maintain. So she began to pray with
her little group that *her minister would change and find the
light*. And had he heard that he was being prayed for in this
way he would have been furious. We would have had two
people confronting each other (or even two factions, since
the little group had grown) each thinking the other had
missed the point, each praying to the same Lord that the
other would change to his vision of what a Christian is. And
then the church organizational life and the pulpit would
have become battle grounds for getting the respective points
of view across. Everyone would be hurt and frustrated and

deeply threatened. And agape love would tiptoe quietly out the door.

Finally, in some cases, in desperation at this growing and uncontrollable "menace," some ministers have rallied their denominational leaders and tried to build a dam across the channel of this stream of "fanaticism" in the church which the people are attributing to the Holy Spirit.

What can be done to prevent this sequence of misunderstandings and painful encounters which can be multiplied by continually larger numbers every year? In the first place, the parishioner could have gone to her minister and thanked him for his patience and prayers over the past ten years. And (if she had known how) she might have used his language by telling him that she was beginning to "become aware of the totality of God's call upon one's priorities, and that she wanted now to begin to study her faith which was at last becoming existentially real for her." But she had no way to know how to do this in his language.

Or the minister might have listened with real interest and joy at one of his flock's new discovery of the gospel message, and then suggested that the two of them stop and give thanks in prayer together for this wonderful new beginning. He could have realized that newly committed lay men and women are not supposed to be articulate like C. S. Lewis or Frederick Buechner. He could have tried to understand that they are filled only with love and a sense of release. He could have seen that most lay people do not have philosophically trained minds; and that when he rejected the *terms* of this woman's theological statement that she could not separate her statement from herself, and only felt *personal* rejection.

One of the causes for this kind of conflict is, in my opinion, a misunderstanding of the practical sequence of consequences which may follow genuine conversion. When any human love relationship becomes deeply personal, and real commitment ensues, there is a period of adjusting to the centering of one's attention and concern from self to another. For some reason this transition always seems to include an almost exclusive preoccupation with the beloved. The best human analogy might be the honeymoon period in marriage. All the happy bride can talk about is "my George." She is convinced that their relationship will somehow miraculously by-pass the otherwise universal problems of marriage. And during this period of rose-colored living she is virtually oblivious of other responsibilities and people. Her elders in the pilgrimage of marriage can only smile and help her adjust to the shocks and surprises as they come and wait for her to pass through to a mature relationship to the world.

In the deep kind of personal Christian commitment the New Testament calls for, a similar phenomenon often seems to take place. All the new Christian can talk about is "Jesus and me." The new love and devotion to the Lord of the church often makes the starry-eyed Christian seem to his minister selfish and oblivious of any social and institutional duties. And for all practical purposes the new convert may not be worth shooting for six months with regard to a meaningful articulation or burden-bearing in the church's program. Paul may have spent several years in this period (Gal. 1:17); Augustine spent months.[1] And during this honeymoon period the new Christian needs encouragement, patience, and help in trying to learn to live in a new Christ-centered life. When such a person does not receive these things, he or she is not likely to go to that minister to find the direction toward maturity as he or she comes out of the honeymoon period and begins to look for the shape of his or her particular obedience in the world.

I think that another of the primary causes for the language and communication barriers between committed lay people and their ordained ministers stems from mistaken ideas about "commitment" and the "ministry." When I was first in the oil business and had become aware that I wanted to know God as He is revealed in Jesus Christ, I started to read books and ask questions about the faith. I began to teach an occasional Sunday school class and became active in the church's program. Before long people would say, "You ought to be a minister." The implication was that if a lay person's commitment and involvement rise to a certain level, he or she will love Christ enough to go to seminary and become an ordained pastor. Ordination, therefore, in the eyes of the average lay person has become a religious

---

[1] *The Confessions of St. Augustine* (New York: E. P. Dutton and Company, Inc., 1951), Book IX, pp. 189 f.

status symbol of total commitment. And some are afraid to make a serious commitment, since they know they are not cut out to be ordained ministers.

I remember that I went to seminary because I wanted to serve God in the fullest way possible—even though I honestly *did not* want to become a parish minister, nor did I feel called to be one. But unknowingly the church has sometimes implied that if you are *really serious* about wanting to serve God totally, this decision is tantamount to a call to the *ordained* ministry. But I do *not* believe this is true—or scriptural. In the earliest New Testament accounts, committed Christians within the fellowship were set aside or ordained for certain special tasks or *functions*. The first deacons were appointed and set apart by the laying on of hands to wait tables (Acts 6:1–6). These men were ordained not because they had reached a certain level of commitment which other Christians had not reached; but they were ordained because someone trustworthy was needed to *wait on the tables*.

I believe this is still true in the Christian community— that men are ordained to preach (for example) not because they are the most committed, but because they have been given certain specialized gifts to be used to help equip God's (equally committed) people for work in His service "to the building up of the body of Christ," the whole church (see Ephesians 4:11 f.). But as long as an ordained pastor feels (even unconsciously) that his or her decision to become ordained and subsequently acquire theological education are signs of a will *more* given to God than that of a committed lawyer or housewife, then that pastor will think of his or her language as the true language of commitment. The pastor will try to educate people to become as he or she is, a trained theologian—instead of helping them to become the *creative business persons and parents and spouses* they were born to be. As an *equipping* minister he will teach them to use *their own* language for Christ's sake rather than try to make them learn his systematic specialized language before he will accept them as being truly committed.

I believe a good many of the misunderstandings between the renewed Christians in our generation and their ordained ministers center around these different views of commitment and ministry, however unconsciously they may be held. But even to solve the thousands of unpleasant personal encounters would not get at the heart of the basic problem here. The question is: can this new wine *ever* be poured into the old wineskins without bursting them?

The option lies with the institutional church. The nature of the new life being breathed into the church today is historically such that it cannot be denied a chance to express itself. Its main stream is based solidly on a scriptural, historical revelation of the mighty acts of God in Christ. These new people are experiencing God's Living Presence together in the person of His Holy Spirit. Above all, these new disciples are mediating carriers of Christ's redeeming love to His world. The building stones of the Protestant and Catholic churches are held together by mortar made from the blood of such people. Unfortunately it seems that they are only recognizable in the flowing robes of the past.

I do not agree with those who have "given up" on the institutional church, as difficult as the situation sometimes seems to be to ministers and laymen. I think there *is* a way. The new wine will not burst the old wineskins *if* the handlers of the old wineskins will receive the new wine and pour it quickly into new skins themselves. This is already happening in many places. And where it is, churches are coming alive with new and deeper involvement with God in His contemporary redeeming activity. Men and women are being reborn to new purpose and loyalty in Christ's love. Such churches are becoming centers for small groups of struggling Christians to come together for worship and training. Many are finding totally new meaning in the sacraments and the Word. Many times such parishes find that their people have come across denominational lines to learn to be God's priesthood of gentle warriors, moving out creatively into the social and moral complexities of our generation.

What goes on in such a parish? What do the new wineskins look like? They are taking many different shapes, but they all seem to have one thing in common: they all call for a kind of dying of our ecclesiastical ego—for those of us who are ministers professionally.[2] We who have been trained to be the central actors in the liturgical drama, played out in the center of the parish stage, have long had

---

[2] I am speaking as a professional writer and speaker.

our people as the paying audience. God has been in the wings whispering the minister's cues. But now the minister is being called on to become the backstage prompter in the wings while his *lay people* play out the drama of contemporary redemption on the larger stage of their homes and communities and the world . . . with God, the author of the drama, as the audience!

This means a drastic rethinking of the term *ministry* (which has been and is being undertaken all around us in the church). The idea of the equipping minister (see Ephesians 4) is becoming a reality in the parishes mentioned above. Pastors are counseling with small struggling groups and individuals about how to study, where to locate resource people, how to find the particular shape of their own obedience in specific moral, ethical and social situations in their vocational worlds. The pastors are having to realize that God did not call His people to be a nation of academically proficient theologians or critical biblical exegetes. They are realizing that at the grass roots level God is not in the academic theologian-producing business. He is in the *life-changing* business![3] And to change men's lives in relationship to Him-

---

[3] This line of thinking is not anti-intellectual or anti-doctrinal. I believe a deeply committed Christian will inevitably study and learn all he can propositionally about his faith. But I am convinced that the *focus* of his life must be on living in relationship with God and His people, rather than on the acquisition of knowledge about these things.

self and to each other, God must be in intimate touch with those who do not know of Him and His love.

Since the professional parish minister today is often not in intimate touch with pagan man where he lives and works, the new missionary and minister of Christ to this generation's vocational, social, and political life must be the *Christian lay person.* This means that the parish minister must love Christ enough to die to the centrality of his role in the church. He must become the coach, the teacher and pastor of the lay persons who will be the new focus of attention in the developing renewal movement of God's people in our time. He must in one sense love Christ more than his own life.

For years people have been saying things like this from the pulpit and in the press, but the parish minister has cynically known from bitter experience that lay people simply have neither been willing nor able to articulate the faith as effective missionaries. But that is just the point. *They are beginning to now!* The problem is that many ministers who have prayed and preached for this are afraid to trust the laymen with the Message for fear that they will somehow misrepresent and oversimplify it. Of *course* we will contaminate the Gospel (as *everyone* does; certainly as between Barth *or* Tillich, for instance, one must have been contaminating it). But God does not primarily need precise orators, he needs channels, lovers! Certainly Christ Himself and Paul *et al* did not fear to trust this message to the theologically untrained people whose lives had been made new through it. Nor in the long run can we.

But what then is the committed Christian's job as a minister (ordained or unordained)? I believe the new wine calls for a revolutionary kind of ministry more profound and exciting than at any time in the past for both lay people and pastors. The lay person must not only share his life and Christ's concerned love in the most complex age in history, but he must learn to help God *reproduce reproducers* for His ministry in the world. This is the third and most penetrating level of sharing Christianity.

This kind of Christian ministry consists of getting together with one or two or twelve people who have already begun to give their wills to God and who are hungry to know Him and His will for their lives. One way to begin is to start meeting at least weekly and spending the time it takes over the weeks and months and years to pour your whole cup into theirs. You share together with the utmost honesty the current problems *you* are having as an individual and as a minister in trying to be wholly Christ's person. You learn to study the Scriptures together (and later devotional classics and perhaps history and theology along with the Bible) relating your study constantly to your personal lives and the practical ways in which the message may be lived out in your own homes and communities. You teach people to lead and teach other people individually or in other small groups. You pray for each other and other people specifically.

You let your life and your concern win you the right to be heard by the church as well as the pagan world. And you, as leader, hold back nothing in your teaching and life.

This seems at first glance the illogical way. Only the greatest ministers have had the perception to overcome the temptation to spend all their time with larger groups. But historically, real spiritual leadership seems to have been passed from person to person individually. Certainly biblical history indicates this. Moses was told to find a man; and Joshua led the people of the next generation in the actual conquering Moses had dreamed of. Elijahs have chosen their Elishas and God has continued to have other mouthpieces in succeeding generations. And in the New Testament, look at the way Paul operated: he always had one or two with him, pouring himself into them, and teaching them to pour themselves into a few others—Timothy, Titus, Aristarchus, Mark—a few in each place, on each journey, into whom he was quietly building the vision of his soul and to whom he was demonstrating how it could be given to others.

In the Galilean life of Christ this principle of ministry is supremely demonstrated. Jesus evidently spent about two-thirds of His active ministry with *twelve men.* And He did not give the twelve a formal education. As Bishop Newbigin has put it, He did not give these twelve a systematized course. "Being with Him they received not so much a formal course of instruction in divine truth as an introduction into the intimacy of His Spirit"[4] . . . of His life with God. Through these twelve and Paul and his disciples, a multiple progression of life changing lives began.

Historians are often amazed that a handful of virtually uneducated men and women by the world's standards, with no social or political connections of importance—no program—no systematic theology or plan—no budget—no mass media (or even the corpus of the New Testament for several hundred years)—could begin transforming a large part of the whole world's concept of the character and purposes of God for men. It is particularly baffling that this one sect burst forth from the empty tomb and began covering the earth. Even acknowledging the tremendously propitious time in history into which Christ came, the development of Christianity is amazing.

But the world did not see Paul on those lonely nights in the wilds of the Tarsus mountains, or in Macedonia, or at Ephesus, often tired from working all day as we do (to call Paul a "lay man" may be considered specious thinking, but he was in the transient home-building business and seemed to consider his lay vocational status an important aspect of his witness—1 Cor. 9), pouring his life with Christ carefully into the souls of Silas and Timothy. Paul was not just preaching a message; he was loving and training the children of a family which was to inherit the earth.

---

[4] Lesslie Newbigin, *The Household of God* (New York: Friendship Press, 1960), p. 62.

But this kind of ministry is so threatening and so revealing that few will try it. It will take time from mass evangelism and financial programs designed for immediate increase in church rolls. And not many people will hear your eloquence. Alone with a few deeply interested men and women, week after week, the holes in the mask of your education will show; and more particularly your own spiritual limitations and weaknesses will be revealed. Some will wander away. But if you are faithful and honest and keep your eyes on Christ and His will, I believe you will begin to experience together a new courage and a communicable enthusiasm, precisely *because* you are free to fail. Your strength and your hope is now in Christ and not in your own spiritual knowledge, ability, and results. As those close around you see the Source of your life and theirs, they will begin to bring others to Christ. And the people these growing Christians bring into God's family will be born at a deeper level than they were, into an increasingly more committed and mature fellowship of men and women who are disciples becoming apostles for Christ.

The point is, if you genuinely want lay renewal in your church, I believe you will have to have somewhere in your own experience a living, growing fellowship of people who are being gently crushed into the wine of new life. This family will be the spiritual home, the true center of Christ's church, into which other people can be brought to be loved and reborn.

As I am completing these thoughts I remember years ago considering the kind of life which might be demanded of me if I made a consciously unreserved commitment of my future to Christ. I saw great specters in my imagination of unpleasant things I would be required to do or be . . . all very pious and grim and a little frightening. Now, years later, I must smile. Because the strange fact of the matter is that when the time has come to say or do some of the things I had feared, I have been compelled to say or do them by a real and joyous desire to do so. Instead of grimness has come the freedom and joy of being able to accept myself as a self-centered sinner being won to Christ . . . day by day.

Finally, I was afraid that if I really cut the cord of the anchor which was tied to myself and began to venture forth in faith, God would send me to the mission field (which would of course mean Africa, India, or some remote place, since Christ said to be His witnesses to "the ends of the earth"—Acts 1:8). But recently I have seen why it is that I have always thought of the "ends of the earth" as some far-off place. I now realize that it is because the *center* of the world has always been *wherever I am*. But where then is the end of the earth from *God's* perspective?

If the heart which beat in Jesus Christ was in any sense the heart which throbs at the center of the universe, then the "ends of the earth" from God's perspective may be wherever the influence from that heartbeat stops—in your own home, your own business, your own congregation.

So it may be that Christ is calling those of us who have tasted of His new wine to stay at home, right where we are, and be wholly His people there. And perhaps for the first time in our lives we will find that we have truly . . . come Home.